D0194329

Your Calling as an Elder

Gary Straub

CHALICE
PRESS
ST. LOUIS, MISSOURI

Biblical quotations, unless otherwise noted, are from the *New Revised Standard Version Bible*, copyright 1989, Division of Christian Education of the National Council of the Churches of Christ in the United States of America. Used by permission. All rights reserved.

Cover design: Wynn Younker
Interior design: Elizabeth Wright
Art direction: Michael Domínguez

This book is printed on acid-free, recycled paper.

Visit Chalice Press on the World Wide Web at
www.chalicepress.com

10 9 8 7 6 5 4 3   05   06   07   08

Library of Congress Cataloging–in–Publication Data

Straub, Gary.
  Your calling as an elder / by Gary Straub.– 1st ed.
     p. cm.
  ISBN 0-8272-4410-X (alk. paper)
  1. Elders (Church officers) 2. Christian Churches (Disciples of Christ)–Government. I. Title.
  BX7326.S77 2003
  253–dc22

                                              2003014885

Printed in the United States of America

Contents

Preface

Elders have always played a "larger than life" role in my life. For instance, Malcolm Crandall, a brick mason by trade and chief elder in the First Christian Church of Williamsport, Pennsylvania, was my church basketball coach when I was a kid. This man molded my soul by his example. My own father, a Marine Corps sergeant and master craftsman in the printing industry, was a men's Bible class teacher and elder in the Christian Church, and laid hands on me when I was ordained. Across the past thirty years of ministry, I have intuitively connected with elders and found grace and strength in their partnership in the gospel. If it weren't for sensible yet visionary elders in every congregation I've ever served, I would have been duck soup!

As I have journeyed through the valleys and shadows of parish life, the encouragement of the elders has been the key to my ministry. This book is my chance to give back. So to all the elders with whom I have had the privilege of standing shoulder to shoulder in the elders' circle, I dedicate this resource. You have my deep and abiding gratitude. I realize now that most of God's good work on this earth is accomplished by elders who have already put in a full day's work by the time they get to church!

In September of 1977, with two years full-time experience as an associate and a newly minted Vanderbilt doctorate, I had just been named senior minister of First Christian Church in Chattanooga, Tennessee. I was overwhelmed! My first official task was to attend the General Assembly in Kansas City, where Dr. John Paul Pack, a beloved former Chattanooga minister, sat me down and preached me the gospel: "You can't succeed in that church without the elders; with them you cannot fail." So we gathered the elders in the living room of Jack and Mavoreen

Mullins, two beloved elders. We frankly discussed the obvious: I couldn't possibly do this without them. After we talked late into the evening, we stood in a circle, joining hands and hearts to pray. That was the beginning of the elders' circle. Over the next five years, we would meet often to puzzle out problems, encourage one another, and pray. In two succeeding decade-long pastorates, I would stand in the elders' circle week after week, month after month, year upon year. In fact, I am still standing in the elders' circle and being sustained in spiritual partnership as we share servant leadership in the congregation.

I have come to appreciate the reasons Paul and Barnabas appointed elders in each congregation they founded to become the leaders on the ground—the grassroots guidance—for God's people. I find, by and large, elders are well-chosen. Oh, there are a few grumps and grouches in every batch, but most elders are possessed by a God-given desire to serve their congregation well, yet they lack the necessary skills and encouragement to translate that desire and dream into spiritual leadership.

The concept of the elders' circle creates and helps order the spiritual life of the congregation. The circle functions as an ongoing spiritual community within the life of the larger community, where elders may practice their faith, witness their growth, learn about leadership, discern direction, deepen prayer life, coordinate their pastoral care, and model the attitudes that will carry the congregation beyond the ordinary. It also places the pastor within that circle as a leader of the leaders or, in the words of Robert Greenleaf, as a servant leader,[1] and first among equals or team coach.

Special thanks to all the elders who eldered me all along the way, whose wise counsel and encouragement I could always count on whether we agreed or disagreed on the topic at hand. I especially thank those who found the courage to open up their lives to me and give me a window into what it is like for them to bear before God the spiritual responsibility of a congregation of

---

[1]Robert K. Greenleaf, *Servant Leadership* (New York: Paulist Press, 1977), 61.

souls, especially those who treated me as a partner and playing coach.

A word of appreciation must be expressed to Bethany Project friends, who prayed this book into being, and to Verna Parrish, who patiently revised my scribbles so many times over the years! Last, but by no means least, I thank Geneva, my best friend and life companion for thirty-five years.

The basic premise of this book is this: The spiritual revitalization we seek for our Disciples congregations begins with the vitality of the elders as spiritual leaders, practicing their faith in community. If there are signs of health, ongoing growth, vitality, and joy within the circle, there is a hopeful future for the congregation. Without this spiritual vision guiding the core spiritual community of the congregation, we are simply shuffling deck chairs on the Titanic.

Gary Straub
First Christian Church
Frankfort, Kentucky

1

Who, Me? An Elder?

When the nominating committee calls, there's a moment of transcendental hesitation on your end of the line. This call is a clear-cut case of mistaken identity: They have asked you to serve as an elder!

But seriously, a flood of emotions hits. You are honored, flattered, and scared. Many elders tell me they feel joy to be invited to serve Christ's church in this capacity, but don't feel worthy. You finally manage to mumble something about how you'd "like to pray about it." Now what? Where do you begin the process of sorting out this decision?

One place I encourage potential elders to start is the listening side of prayer. How about entering into a season of discernment, during which you sift through questions designed to illuminate some of the spiritual considerations as you search out God's call on your life? The actual practice need not be cumbersome. Simply set aside a small daily time block (fifteen to twenty minutes) for perhaps a week. You may find it helpful to develop a simple ritual, such as sitting in your favorite chair and lighting a candle as a sign of your intention to welcome the light of Christ as you present yourself to the Presence to receive whatever illumination God might be so gracious as to offer. If you are "on the run" schedule-wise, you may elect to devote a particular stretch of road you are driving to quiet discernment, setting aside these miles as consecrated to the listening side of prayer (and paying attention to driving!). Whatever the physical arrangements, the spiritual intention is clear: to purposefully offer yourself in a particular time and space to God. Here are twenty sets of questions that may help you discern your answer to the call.

Discerning the Call to Eldership

(An inventory for spiritual self-examination)

1. **Joy.** Can I name the joy in this possibility?
2. **Advice.** What does my family think? Got any words of wisdom from longtime friends who know me all too well?
3. **Negative Impact.** Is there anything in my past that if publicly known might negatively impact the congregation (arrests, felonies, lawsuits, violations, accusations, what else)? How have I resolved these matters within my own soul? Would it help to disclose them in confidential conversation with a trusted spiritual adviser?
4. **Unfinished Business.** Are there any emotional, spiritual, or personal issues that are substantially unfinished in my soul that might hinder my ability to serve wholeheartedly? Do I know what my "hot button" issues are that consistently skew my perspective? Am I willing to name, dig out, address, and resolve these matters?
5. **Spiritual Gifts.** Do I know my own spiritual gifts well enough to know how my strengths might complement the congregation and its needs at this time in its life? Am I willing to collaborate and serve out of my spiritual gifts for the common good of the congregation?
6. **Scandal.** Is there anything in my life as I examine it that could create a scandal to the gospel and give unbelievers just the excuse they need to disrespect the church? How do I deal with aspects of my own "not-so-pretty" personality that may arise from time to time?

7. **Recovery.** If I am in recovery for an addiction, have I been walking that path long enough to develop a mature perspective? Is my life "in order"?

8. **Personal Disclosures.** Are there any matters that I have not confessed before God and humankind that could negatively affect my capacity to serve effectively?

9. **Pastoral Relationship.** Do I have a positive regard for the pastor beside whom I'll serve? Do I have a collegial spirit with current pastoral leadership? Am I willing to lead and be led by my pastor?

10. **Unyieldedness.** Since eldering is a major commitment to ongoing spiritual growth, are there any hindrances or barriers to my spiritual growth I am unwilling to yield to God? Do I have any major or minor issues that might become a stumbling block to my leadership? What about my "pet peeves" and "hobby horses"?

11. **Holy Spirit.** Have I developed a mature understanding of and intimate communion with the Holy Spirit that allows me to respond with consistent sensitivity to the guidance of God in my life? Have I gotten past being "spooked" by the Spirit to appreciate the energy and strength of Paul's statement in Philippians 4:13?

12. **Devotional Life.** Have I devoted myself on a daily basis to those habits and practices of faith (especially prayer and reading scripture) that will sustain my spiritual service over the long haul, especially through times of controversies, dry spells, grief, upheaval, frustration, and aggravation that mark some seasons in the life of my congregation?

13. **Fears.** Are any of my hesitancies about accepting this call fear-based? Will I allow God's perfect love to cast out fear so I can discern the deeper call beneath the anxiety?

14. **Problems or Satisfactions.** What do I imagine my biggest problems with being an elder might be? What might be the most spiritually satisfying aspect?

15. **Facing Myself.** Since it is inevitable that eldering will bring me face-to-face with my own faults, flaws, foibles, frailties,

and finitude (to say nothing of my weaknesses), what do I imagine will be the outcome of my facing the shadow side of my own human nature?

16. **Expectation.** Is there anything I expect will happen to me spiritually in that moment when I am installed or ordained to the office of elder?

17. **Example.** How will I deal with the discomfort of being "looked up to" as a spiritual example? How comfortable am I with the spiritual reality of my own Christlikeness?

18. **Core Faith.** Have the essential core matters of the ancient faith been settled within my soul in such a way that I can embody them in teaching—both formally and informally? Do I know the faith, both inside and out? (intellectually and experientially)? Can my soul bear the weight of being a bearer of Christ's light?

19. **Legacy.** What might my spiritual legacy as an elder to this congregation look like? Am I willing to begin now doing those things that will lead to such a blessing or legacy?

20. **Vision.** Can I gather into my own spirit any sense of the spiritual vision of our congregation's mission; and what of that vision is mine to own and carry out? How does my personal mission statement fit with the mission of the congregation at this time?

I invite you to work through this list, examining your own soul and adding your own questionings to these. I encourage you to learn to love the questions as well as the answers. Carry your questions around awhile and open them out before God often. You may wish to invite a trusted friend or two to pray over the same twenty questions in their prayers and meet together later to compare notes. You may want to make a daylong retreat dedicated to the specific purpose of discerning a call. There is no substitute for setting aside a block of time in your favorite place of prayer and simply waiting before God. Any time and space you consecrate by your intention can become a temple for meditation—a cathedraled moment! When you are done rehearsing before God all your reasons and reservations, hollow out some space at the deepest levels of your being for only listening. Just being present for God, honoring and appreciating the divine Presence will place you in a place where you may hear a call.

Why on Earth Did They Ask Me to Be an Elder?

Beyond the surprise and sense of unworthiness, many who are asked to serve in this office sincerely wonder why they were chosen. Here is a possibility: The congregation sees in your soul those qualities of spiritual leadership necessary for churches to survive and thrive in ministry. Eldering is not a popularity contest or a political office with constituencies to poll and voters to impress. Nor is eldering an opportunity to inflict our own personal pet peeve issues on the congregation. The church already has a mission around the Great Commission: to win, disciple, baptize, and serve; to teach obedience to Christ; to remember and represent the Presence of the One who is ever with us (Mt. 28:19).

We have our work cut out for us. The question is: Are we cut out for this work? In the congregation's considered wisdom, you are. Don't spend a lot of time second-guessing or underestimating that.

Laying aside any self-deprecating humor about "those nominators really scraping the bottom of the barrel," your first assignment is to discover the joy of this call. After all, people who have known you for some time and watched you operate in some difficult situations and circumstances find in you the spiritual gifts and graces needed to lead Christ's church. The question becomes: How can I lend my strength to this quest?

You have been selected as an elder because you cannot seem to help yourself: You already are one! I encourage nominating committees or call teams to look out across the congregation and ask this question: "Who is already elding?" Elders just "eld." That's just what they do, because that's who they are. In the eyes of your local nominating team, you consistently and gladly give yourself to spiritual matters and community concerns in the life of your home congregation as well as the broader church. Your willingness to wade in the deep waters while others are content to play in the shallow end of the pool helped the nominating committee exclaim: "Look, there's one!" In other words, eldering is both "being" and "doing."

Disciples eldership is both an office you are elected to and a way of life you have chosen to live before God. Elders are much more than people who are selected to fill slots on the communion team schedule! Elders are part of a living tradition of faithful persons who keep saying yes to the heart of God. As you live out your "yes to God," the actual duties of the office are not at all burdensome to you. You bear them with a lightness of spirit and begin to discover that your soul would gladly bear much more than any church constitution might require! As a disciple and follower of Jesus Christ, you are already committed to a lifelong learning process that increasingly conforms you to the image of Christ and increasingly confirms Christ's image in you. So this new call to serve as elder may come at a good time in your life, confirming your chosen spiritual vocation and providing clarity about the next decisive step on this journey.

A Word to Newly Ordained, First-time Elders

Congratulations, you have just joined the ranks of those who for more than five thousand years have faithfully answered a divine call on their lives. The first biblical reference to elders appears to date back to the time of the exodus. In the wilderness story of Exodus 18, Moses was exhausted, depleted, and weary of advising and overseeing the tribes and adjudicating their daily disputes. He was well advised by Jethro, his father-in-law, to select key elders to assume this role. Ever since Moses took Jethro's advice and appointed elders to guide, guard, and lead, a portion of God's Spirit has rested on those who honor this calling. You have no doubt been invited into this leadership circle because your congregation sees something of God's worth and glory in the way you conduct your life and serve the kingdom.

Some reflection of glory came to rest on the elders Moses appointed as they ate and drank before the Lord, on the mountain of God (Ex. 24:11). A similar reflection of the glory of God is portrayed in the New Testament, as a special benediction of the Spirit resting on the local elders who were left "in charge" of the missionary churches that Paul and Barnabas founded across Asia Minor (Acts 20). When hands are laid on you to ordain you to this elder calling, you may well sense this same weight of glory inspiring and empowering you.

A Word to Returning Elders

Congratulations! You have just rotated back on the church board, and the mantle of leadership falls on your shoulders once again to feed and lead God's flock (1 Pet. 5). The grace of the Great Shepherd will surely guide you as you seek simply and humbly to provide for your flock what God provides you. As you anticipate the weight and burden of problems facing the congregation in your next term of service, don't let the despair of that "lonesome leadership feeling" overwhelm you. Of course you will bear the weight of decisions affecting the spiritual welfare of the congregation, but you are not alone. God has given you companions for this part of the journey. The bread and the cup will also sustain you in the presence of Christ. You will find friendship and spiritual kinship in the elders' circle. This is a good time to reaffirm the spiritual bond—the yoke of partnership—you share with your pastor. It is also a season to seek a renewed vision around the question of how the call of God rests on you for this season or passage of the church's life. In other words: Why you? Why now? The dedication of your spiritual gifts and energies could play a major role in the next "defining moment" in the congregation's history. Do not modestly rule this possibility out.

2

The Elder in the New Testament

What kind of person accepts the office of elder? We might kiddingly answer, "Only a glutton for punishment!" or "someone who actually enjoys being stoned to death by popcorn!" Seriously, though, an elder is one who already bears the work of Christ deeply in his or her heart. Here's why. Just as members of the congregation often still put their pastors on pedestals (even though they have good reason to know better), so they often put their elders on pedestals too. Generally speaking, congregations expect their elders to be the kind of spiritual people they wish they had the time (or discipline) to be. As an elder, you are expected to be a "real, down-to-earth, yet spiritual" person. The bottom line: You are called to manifest integrity of character. You are invited to reflect and embody the Christ Spirit. Elders serve best by being what Henri Nouwen has called "the living reminder" in your local congregation. In his book by that title, Nouwen teaches us: "There has been, and only ever will be *one* ministry in the whole history of the world–that of Jesus Christ. All any of us ever do is serve as the living reminders of his one, true ministry."[1] As

---

[1] Henri J.M. Nouwen, *The Living Reminder: Service and Prayer in Memory of Jesus Christ* (New York: Seabury Press, 1977), 27.

Disciples elders, being a living reminder is our best and only work.

In a "Chat with Chet" column in the *Disciple* magazine years ago, Chester Sillars put it quite succinctly: "Elders must be the best persons in the church, no matter how you measure that!" While it is true that different eras of the church's life call forth varying degrees of appreciation for different spiritual qualities, excellence in leadership that reflects the mind of Christ is clearly what Chet had in mind. Although I have long since lost Chet's original article, I still regularly offer his column's "Six Characteristics of Elders" to call teams and/or nominating committees.

Here are the six characteristics Chet uplifted: *First,* elders must be deeply spiritual persons who practice what they preach. *Second,* elders should be faithful persons who consider the service of God their highest honor. *Third,* elders must embody sacrificial stewardship by their own example. *Fourth,* elders should be enjoyable persons who are actually a blessing to be around. *Fifth,* elders are persons who make it their business to know the inner workings of the worldwide church beyond the local congregation. *Sixth,* elders are people whose loyalty to the Lord is not only self-evident but also laced with deep humility.

The Question of Qualification

In the body of literature currently available on elder leadership, I recommend two books that discuss this matter of qualification in excellent detail. Edwin Linberg and Rod Parrott's *The Ministry of Elders*[2] will fill in the necessary scholarship. Peter Morgan's *Disciples Eldership*[3] is the most recent comprehensive overview of the work of elder available. Both books will be enormous practical help to local congregational leaders inquiring about this matter of qualification.

---

[2]Rodney L. Parrott and Edwin Linberg, *The Ministry of Elders: A Handbook for Elders in Congregations of the Christian Church* (Claremont and Berkeley: Oikodome Publications, 1990).

[3]Peter M. Morgan, *Disciples Eldership: A Quest for Identity and Ministry* (St. Louis: Christian Board of Publication, 1993).

Perhaps because of our tendency to feel the weight and gravity of the office as well as a sense of personal unworthiness, discussions around the issue of biblical qualification are sometimes aimed at seeking grounds for disqualification. The question of "how literally" to take the apostolic teachings in the pastoral epistles often becomes a sort of litmus test for the larger question of biblical inspiration. Because there are snake pits on both sides of these interpretation questions, I suggest our practice in calling elders be: Don't just take these biblical standards literally; take them seriously! Ponder them long and hard. Question the original meanings. Study the context and history. Dig out the grammar. Spare no expense to gain the best understanding you can possess. Be satisfied that you are what Paul calls "a worker who has no need to be ashamed, rightly explaining the word of truth" (2 Tim. 2:15). When you complete your exhaustive studies, the toughest task will still be to apply the interpretive wisdom: How does this revealed truth fit the life and leadership of the potential elder who is before us as a candidate?

Over the years, I have come to understand the biblical statement of qualifications as signposts and cautions (not unlike the Old Testament divination tools of Urim and Thummum) that serve to guide the nominating committee to the right person for the right time of leadership in that local congregation's life. That old line from the deliberations of the Jerusalem Council when they were deciding what standards would be required in order for a Jewish convert to be considered "truly Christian" comes to mind: "It seemed good to the Holy Spirit and to us…" (Acts 15:28). When the final benediction is pronounced over our work as nominating committees, we must ultimately trust our most learned discernments to that strange sense of "settled peace" that comes to rest on the life of the one we have chosen. This is what the Quakers call "the infusion of divine light" or "the sense of the meeting." This language points to a "consensus in the Spirit" that might carry at least as much weight as literal translations.

Here is a brief interpretive summary of the biblical qualifications for elder leadership. Fourteen positive characteristics and six negative ones are enumerated in scripture. Words in parentheses reflect differing Bible translations.

Fourteen Positive Characteristics of Elders

1. Hospitable. Titus 1:8

This characteristic speaks to the natural spiritual role of becoming a befriender of those who are in need. It has nothing to do with being an off-the-charts extrovert on some psychological scale. Whether one's personality type is quiet or loud, a genial generosity that witnesses warmth and authentic approachability is the key here. Perhaps Romans 15:7 says it best: "Welcome one another...just as Christ has welcomed you, for the glory of God!"

2. Lover of Goodness. Titus 1:8

We are looking for an enthusiastic spirit of passion that embraces those things that are wholesome and positive (Phil. 4:8) in life and in the church family. This attitude builds healthy consensus and embodies the zest and joy of God's life alive in ours. People who have no sense of humor—about their own problems, to say nothing of the faults and foibles of others—have no business being elders! Our sins of cynicism melt away when we devote ourselves wholeheartedly to that which is good. Enthusiasm for this good is contagious in church life!

3. Just (Upright). Titus 1:8

Here we have reference to that quality of fair-mindedness that has its sights set on nothing less than the church as the living parable of Isaiah's peaceable kingdom, or Amos' mighty river of justice flowing down. There's something highly positive about not being willing to compromise on matters of human treatment or dignity and being unafraid to say so! Elders who live by the vision of God's justice may not find prophetic boldness in such matters their natural style, but are nonetheless able to step up to the plate and give witness to the reason for their faith (1 Pet. 3:15).

4. Holy (Devout). Titus 1:8

An elder is someone who takes seriously and submits to the inner process of personal sanctification, without falling into the trap of perfectionism or spiritual narcissism. There is a deep connection here with the concept and practice of surrender, yielding as much of ourselves as we can command to as much of Christ's spirit as we can understand. Health, wholeness, and well-being are integrally related as we grow toward God's shalom in our own soul, with the goal being conformity to the sufferings and power of Christ (Phil. 3:4–11).

5. Self-controlled. Titus 1:8

This refers to the ability to exercise judicious and appropriate restraint without giving vent to frustration in ways that do disservice to the gospel. Self-control has to do with allowing God's spirit to develop appropriate and healthy boundaries within the soul as restraints against impulsive actions and reactions. The moral strength to curb sinful desires, habits, attitudes, and appetites is also a fruit of the Spirit abiding within (Gal. 5:22). The ability to simply ignore the door when temptation knocks is an enormous grace, but letting Christ answer the door may be an even greater grace.

6. Sober-minded (Prudent). Titus 1:8

An elder is one who chooses to live centered in God, and therefore not excessively distracted by ego attachments to emotions, earthly allegiances, or unworthy and lesser alliances. This attitude renders a soul sane, sensible, temperate, and discreet. In other words, someone who knows that being an elder is not "all about me." The selfish ego is "dead, buried, and out-of-the-way" so as to attend to God's business cleanly, clearly, single-mindedly, and without distraction (1 Pet. 5:8).

7. Holder of the Word. Titus 1:9

An elder has the capacity to receive God's word into his or her soul and embrace it lovingly–like Mary, "pondering these things in her heart"—with a view toward surrendering one's own desires and outcomes to the truth of God revealed. First Thessalonians 4:4 speaks of being a fit vessel or an ark where the covenant may dwell. Being a worthy container (2 Cor. 4:7) of the Word seems to carry with it the implication of willingness to "serve the Word." Acts 6:2 urges becoming an embodier of the Word.

8. Orderly. 1 TIMOTHY 3:2

Attending to God's business requires that elders speak a word of order to the chaos that breaks loose in church life from time to time. Being able to delineate clear boundaries for appropriate behavior becomes necessary. Monitoring and honoring the process of decision-making and knowing when and how to "color inside the lines" help others who are experiencing chaos receive the gift of structure when their world may be falling to pieces. The ability to offer a firm yet gracious word of limitation, or a positive word of appropriate permission, is critical to congregational peace. Sometimes elders have to put on the striped referee shirt, blow the whistle, and call fouls. This is more than just "helping others play by the rules"; it is being ordered interiorly by the rule of Christ.

9. Grave. TITUS 2:2 (KJV)

This does not mean "one foot in it!" Elders who can enjoy a hearty laugh that is not at someone else's expense, are a refreshing, "pick-me-up" tonic, and fun to be around. Knowing when to treat a concern in the life of the church with high seriousness and all due dispatch is simply recognizing that when someone else is hurting is not the time for jokes and frivolity. Your flock knows you honor their dignity and their spiritual needs when you take them seriously. Pain, distress, and need must be taken seriously. To balance this, we seek the corresponding grace that can say with a straight face to the habitual whiners and complainers in every congregation: "You may be assured the elders will give this matter the attention it deserves!" Maybe elders, like G. K Chesterton's angels, can fly because they take themselves lightly!

10. Able to Teach. Titus 1:9

Elders should be able to preach and teach the gospel, even according to Francis of Assisi, "using words if necessary"! The teaching gift does not refer to attainment of a graduate degree in education or theology, but simply the discernment to recognize the gospel whenever and wherever it is embodied or spoken. Through their collective wisdom, the elders carry around in their consciousness the living canon. This means being embodiers as well as imparters of the "faith that was once for all entrusted to the saints" (Jude 3). The elders consistently keep on delivering the gospel to the saints. This requires a teachable spirit, which translates into enormous inner openness to God. Maintaining this steady willingness to be tutored by the Spirit requires a healthy measure of spiritual maturity. "Keeping the faith" is critical if generations yet to come are to have any faith at all to keep! A teachable and teaching spirit is the elder's spiritual legacy to the congregation.

11. Blameless. Titus 1:6

This characteristic need not be misconstrued as faultlessness or sinless perfection. The expectation of perfectionism is clearly the deadliest form of self-abuse. Dealing with one's own shadow side in a way that keeps words and deeds "in bounds" and does not bring any negative impact to the reputation of the gospel is the point. Another interpretation might suggest: not being overtaken in any glaring insufficiencies in morality or character. What rules this elder's spirit or is the controlling interest of this elder's life? By the grace God gives, elders learn to live above any reproach, accusation, or complaint that might be leveled, whether legitimate or just those "sour grape" aspersions that often make the best whine!

12. Married Only Once. Titus 1:6

The primary meaning, stated positively, reflects a loving and gracious fidelity within the bonds of marriage. Faithfulness in marriage is a reflection of the character of our covenant-keeping

God. Integrity here means living out the honoring of one's marital vows to one's spouse in practical ways that include speaking and acting consistently with the blessing of this sacred commitment. In this day of fast-track divorce within a culture that often practices "serial monogamy," an elder's marriage vows should be kept in a way that reflects positively the biblical witness to household order and divine intention. As this is interpreted in the practice of most Disciples congregations, it does not mean that anyone who has ever suffered a divorce is automatically disqualified from the privilege of office, nor does it even remotely mean that single adults are excluded from consideration. It does mean that the unique circumstances of a person's life have been weighed carefully in the best collective discernment available, and that the elder's marital status creates no public scandal that would reflect negatively on the congregation or the gospel.

13. Children Who Are Believers. Titus 1:6

The spiritual duty of every Christian parent includes passing on the faith by both words and example so that children naturally come to confirm and claim the faith their parents have raised them to receive. Paul's admonition (Eph. 6:1–4) for children to obey their parents is also balanced with the warning that parents are not to provoke their children to anger. We all recognize that hormones may rage out of control at some point in the teen-raising process, as kids carve out their own destiny and confirm it by their choices. The consideration here is not to impose some unrealistic standard that "every elder's child must be Goody Two-shoes," but that the elder's own attempt to maintain and restore appropriate order to the family system be spiritually and emotionally healthy, and in keeping with biblical principles. Whether the results produced are totally effective (or not) is more a matter for prayer than conjecture and judgment.

14. Good Reputation. Titus 1:6

Let the word on the street about this elder be: "unimpeachable!" The call is to a shining spiritual integrity that is transparent and at once obvious. We're talking about sincerity in the original Latin sense of "without wax." In New Testament times, clay pots were advertised in marketplaces as *sine-cera,* that is, without wax. This meant no wax was applied to cover the flaws of the potter's wheel or firing oven so that the vessel might appear to be of "first quality" even though it was in fact a reject or "factory-second." Elders do not attempt to mask or cover up imperfections in a way that could be construed as "phony or hypocritical." In fact, there is a radical translucence about their lives. What you see is what you get. This allows the light of Christ to radiate, even through the inevitable faults, flaws, and foibles of the personality. Being "for real" is a good start for building a reputation that represents the gospel.

Six Negative Traits

Disciples church culture these days highly values acceptance and tolerance. While these virtues are priceless, sometimes in our desire to be all-inclusive we do our flock a disservice if we do not at least slow down for these scriptural "caution flags." There are substantial, well-founded, historical reasons to carefully reconsider persons who have already developed something of a reputation along these six negative patterns. The time to weigh these matters confidentially with the persons themselves is *before* they are called to elder leadership. Perhaps this is why Paul advised that we "not lay hands suddenly upon anyone." These six attitudes or dispositions were known to cause unity problems in the life of the early church. The point is: Elders need to exhibit balanced spiritual maturity that allows them to contribute their unity to the bond of peace that holds at the core of the congregation. The reputational wisdom of every elder needs to be part of the solution instead of being part of the problem! Of course, we are all part of the problem, which is why Christ died. But the truth is that the progress of each elder leader's sancti-fication will be the subject of congregational scrutiny sooner or later. So why not sooner?

1. Not a Brawler (Violent). Titus 1:7

The reference here is to persons who are habitually argumentative to the point of developing a warlike attitude or "siege mentality." This may be some indication of also being given to grudges and carrying around chips on the shoulder, or a long memory for slights and hurts–the wounding by minutiae. This might also involve indulging in "an attitude" whereby one cannot resist offering or responding to digs and barbs and side-comments that only stir the pot of controversy and keep the congregation in turmoil. People who habitually pick fights will have great difficulty with "making every effort to maintain the unity of the Spirit in the bond of peace" (Eph. 4:3).

2. Not Self-willed (Arrogant). Titus 1:7

"Overbearing to the point of being a control freak" comes to mind in today's lingo. Consistently insisting on taking the stance of "my way or the highway" creates an unavoidable adversarial atmosphere that keeps this particular ego at the center of the storm of most congregational controversy. Some personalities feed on this kind of excitement and need this kind of energy to feel alive. Although these are often the kind of folks who "get things done," careful consideration should be given to the psychological price somebody in the church family system will pay. People who cannot resist the temptation to bulldoze, get their own way, and then gloat, and who will not unselfishly choose to keep their ego in check when such self-control serves the common good of the congregation, are generally not well served by the offer of a position of spiritual leadership as a reward for "results."

3. Not Soon Angry (Quick-tempered). Titus 1:7

A person who has low impulse controls, along with little desire to discipline or even monitor and rein in impulses when they strike, will predictably indulge in angry words and reactions that create congregational chaos. This "low flash point" will likely serve to contaminate the community with negative feelings. This is not to say it is inappropriate to be angry in church. After all, Jesus was! However, his wrath worked the righteousness of God. Our anger will most likely work trouble unless it is grounded in scripture and holy boldness against oppression and other indignities consistent with the character of God. We're not talking about having a temper, but asking: Is it under God's control? Consider the question God asked Jonah in this regard (Jon. 4:4). Leaders who nurse anger and can't let go are impaired in ways that inflict damage and keep trouble brewing. Anger is like nitroglycerin: it can either heal a heart or blow up a bridge, and elders who haven't submitted their anger to the Spirit are loose canons!

4. Not Greedy. Titus 1:8

There's a fine line most churches learn to walk internally between the way we "run church in a businesslike manner" and "turning church into a business." The bottom line is not cash or a profit motive or even efficiency. Leaders who co-opt the central purpose of the church with constant cautionary-but-controlling fears often allow money concerns to vitiate the vision. Elders who choose a lifestyle that is "unhooked" from heavy-duty consumerism help balance the "need or greed" equation. Perhaps this is best described by its opposite– giving wholehearted permission to the church's mission and empowering this consuming vision with generous support and encouragement. Elders who understand the church is in business to give itself away are not always trying to save some manna for tomorrow's breakfast. Leaders who are unwilling to unhook from this addiction will hinder spiritual progress.

5. Not a Novice. 1 Timothy 3:6

Perhaps because American Disciples operate in a democratic cultural context, we may be inclined to give candidates for elder equal consideration without factoring in qualification and proven experience. Could this be more of a cultural bias than a biblical principle? The church is not essentially a democratic institution.

The church is a theocracy, ruled by the presence and power of Christ in our midst. Therefore, the practice of voting on everything, where majority rules and everyone is given equal voice and vote, may need further reflection. For instance, nobody runs his or her family in a strictly democratic way. The parents would be outvoted, and ice cream might become the vegetable for every meal. While we may adapt the democratic principles as a guideline, they are not the guiding principle! The reign of God in our midst and enhancing the in-breaking of the kingdom are our ruling principles. When it comes to selecting those who will guide our faith community's destiny, the greatest weight should fall on those who have the most consistent experience in the Christian way of life. The elder's witness to truth applied in real-life situations is highly esteemed in the process of discernment. This is not to say, "All elders must have gray hair," but it is to say, "Preference is given to mature and proven (though not perfect) faith." The question is often: How much experience is "enough"? Weight needs to be given to steadfast faithfulness under pressure, remembering that none of the New Testament elders had any experience eldering in previous congregations!

6. Not Addicted to Wine. TITUS 2:3

Some read this to mean "never given any wine!" (as in teetotaler). More likely, this reference is a spiritual caution regarding those whose lives are dominated by addictions. We know that addictions—unacknowledged, unchecked, and untreated—contaminate a person's thinking process, compromise clear-minded decisions, and make for relationships that have boundary problems. This need not mean that all persons who have ever been in twelve-step treatment should be automatically eliminated. These persons often develop an abiding spirituality the church would do well to tap. However, those whose sobriety has not stood the test of time and the review of twelve-step peers might need to be tempered a bit more and given more time to mature in other leadership roles before they are asked to bear the full weight of eldership.

The Biblical Duties of an Elder

As we read scripture and try to build a profile of the work of elders, we find at least fourteen responsibilities that are specifically mentioned as duties of the office.

1. Take Heed. ACTS 20:28

This line may be variously interpreted: "Keep watch, pay attention, beware, be on the lookout, don't let your guard down." This is a caution to be humbly cognizant of the salient and unsavory features of one's own shadow side, that is, those areas of temptation, weakness, and vulnerability that blindside us and render us almost helpless before sin and cause us to fall. This dark side, unsurrendered to God's Spirit, can be our downside and cause even those who have won others to the faith to be disqualified (1 Cor. 9:27).

2. Take Heed of the Flock. ACTS 20:28

Here's an encouragement to stand watch, be alert without paranoia, stand guard against any form of spiritual endangerment that might be lurking to lure away or pick off unsuspecting members. While 1 Peter 5:8 seems to have the evil one's roaring, wolflike nature in mind, Paul seems to recognize that false teaching can seduce souls under elders' care (2 Tim. 4:3).

3. Receive the Charge of the Holy Spirit. ACTS 20:28

Exercise an openhearted receptivity to whatever gifts and graces the Spirit might be offering an individual elder to equip the church for a particular season of struggle or service. This may well be a special infilling of the indwelling Spirit for a service assignment or prayer empowerment given to guide the shepherds of the flock in special intercession. Hollowing out a space for the Spirit requires receptivity and surrender.

4. Feed the Flock. ACTS 20:28

Overseeing means the capacity to watch over, spot trends, and make certain that the basic spiritual needs of the flock are satisfied. This could well extend to concerns for a balanced diet. Although not all elders are gifted in the areas of teaching and Christian nurture, all are nevertheless charged with paying attention to the ways and means whereby the souls in their care are being shaped and formed.

5. Watch Over and Protect the Flock. ACTS 20:29, 31

Practicing sentry-type vigilance over the congregation anticipates spiritual dangers in various deceptions and disguises. This kind of guardianship may necessitate the ability to offer an admonition, issue a warning, provide strong encouragement, pay attention to potential dangers without becoming alarmist, and even occasionally call for an old-fashioned wake-up call. This prophetic role, after the fashion of Ezekiel 2, is not for the fainthearted.

6. Help the Weak. ACTS 20:35

An elder's reach extends not only to the comfortable middle of the congregation where our friends are and it is easy to be their shepherd but also to the fringe of the flock, to notice and connect with persons who may well need assistance, but will not ask. To put it another way, elders have a "holy spirit" role with those who are weak and hurting, to come along beside them and serve as comforter, advocate, guide, and friend (Jn. 14:25–27). Will this kind of caring be inconvenient? Inevitably! Will these needs be messy? Always! Bear Romans 15:1 in mind. The words of Paul in Philippians 2:5–11 about Jesus' servant spirit also help. If you have not yet memorized this passage, you may wish to do so; it is the heart of your spiritual practice of eldering.

7. Give. ACTS 20:35

Elders are stewards of the mysteries of God and household managers in God's economy. Is it safe to assume that you and the other elders in your congregation have matured in your own philosophy of giving beyond resenting appropriate guidance from the pulpit about money? Such reactivity has a cumulative negative effect on the congregation's willingness. Giving is one area in which elders need not delegate all the theological talk about money to the pulpit. Are the elders and pastors mutually accountable to one another when it comes to the ministry of money and their personal witness? Elders who are both leading by personal stewardship example and finding ways to testify to God's faithfulness within the congregation are invaluable. Costly and sacrificial giving, done in a spirit of gratitude and gladness wins the day! When was the last time the elders stepped up to the challenge of examining their personal stewardship before one another? Let's do something creative here, and not simply fill the air with unhelpful exhortations: "You ought, you should, you know you need to!" Let's face the fact that many in our congregations are far more willing to be spiritually led by the tithing example than we are to lead!

It is well past time for Disciples elders to step up to the joy of tithing. If you are not already tithing and thinking of your tithing as a floor for your giving—not a ceiling—then I urge you to reconsider tithing as part of your elder example! If you are not at least growing year by year in your percentage of giving toward the goal of a tithe as a milestone and stepping-stone, not a millstone, I urge you to reconsider your calling! If you are offended by the challenge of these words, please consider the gravity and joy of the kingdom cause. Perhaps a starting point could be simply asking the question: How long has it been since you have undertaken an audacious audit of your personal level of financial stewardship and asked the hard questions? Begin with: Does the amount I offer God represent any element of sacrifice; or is this amount more related to "my fair share"—like a United Way pledge?

Our churches will not follow us anywhere we are not willing to lead. When it comes to choosing the next three elders in your congregation, in addition to the usual criteria, consider sending in someone who practices the tithe as a biblical benchmark (i.e., a floor, not a ceiling). Watch this make a difference in the overall commitment level of your congregation. It only takes a little leaven to make the whole loaf rise.

8. Tend the Flock. 1 PETER 5:2

Elders are the resident, grassroots, and pastoral caregivers of the congregation. Tending the flock is an image for routine watchfulness for the needs and concerns of the body of Christ. One concrete way elders may demonstrate love and care for the flock is by learning their names. This may seem too elemental for an elaborate shepherding system, but nothing whispers "I care" like knowing a person's name. Nothing glares "I don't care enough" like not knowing names.

People will forgive you of colossal errors and embarrassing bungles. They will think it's funny and appreciate your effort. However, if you, as an elder, don't get your flock's names right or apologize until you finally do, they won't really believe you care yet. Tending the flock begins at home: memorizing names, reviewing the pictorial directory, using word associations, drilling yourself until you can smile and your member's name rolls off your tongue. We all need the blessing of our name being called. Most often, God's call comes to us through the repetition of our name. So get your "tending the flock" efforts off to a solid start. Once we have mastered the names, we are ready to explore learning about the flock's needs through conversation that leads to intercession.

9. Exercise Oversight. 1 PETER 5:2

This speaks to the tremendous need for leaders to develop a simple, straightforward, proactive style that does not wait for disaster to strike before anything is said or done. Too often, elders end up doing "damage control," instead of anticipating and moving forward, being prepared to meet the need before it becomes a crying need and hurts have already begun to accumulate. Elders are leaders who possess the power of initiative, who do not stand around hemming and hawing and wondering, When is the pastor going to do something about this? Elders step up to offer themselves in service of the need. When someone is "acting out rather badly," elders don't wait for the preacher to get home to deal with it. They face the problem, lay claim to their spiritual leadership responsibility, and draw an appropriate boundary, while offering grace at the same time. Elders team up with their pastors to offer creative solutions, work ahead to anticipate situations where spiritual guidance will be needed, and lay groundwork. Simply put: Elders are the "designated adults" of the church family.

10. Don't Lord It over the Flock. 1 PETER 5:3

Here is an exhortation that is astonishing, given the cultural context of Roman world domination. Heavy-handedness and dictatorial methods only create resentment and rebellion. Demanding the authority to be heard is nowhere near as effective as earning it by authenticity.

If your eldership consistently demonstrates that you are a "real, down-to-earth person" who has spiritual "ups and downs" like everybody else, yet you are wanting to reach out beyond yourself in a genuine and unselfish way, people will definitely figure this out and follow your lead. Only your transparent honesty will ever give you any authenticity. Lead out of the power of your spiritual influence. It's the only kind of power by which any of us can ever lead anyway.

11. Be an Example to the Flock. 1 PETER 5:3

Your inner attitude as an elder creates the atmosphere within the climate of the congregation that makes your example a powerfully effective witness. Perhaps Francis of Assisi said it best: "Preach the gospel at all times—use words if necessary!" (Yes, it bears repeating.) Let your personal integrity do your talking. Don't look now, but members of the congregation are already studying your life. The most positive attribute you have to lead with is your attitude. Be a prototype of what you are talking about. If there is a simple, daily, and practical consistency between your "walk" and your "talk," people will take notice and you have gained a hearing for the gospel's witness in your life. Whenever a disparity or inconsistency arises (and it will), don't let the matter drift until the question of hypocrisy arises. Be an example here too. Face up, 'fess up, and keep walking in the light of the Lord

(1 Jn. 1:9). Let your integrity for always being counted on to remain open to the Spirit's conviction and guidance be the heart of your example. Live so others can imitate you as you follow Christ. There is excellent biblical precedent for this in Philippians 3:17. Humbly accept that your example is already tarnished by the fact that it is not a perfect one. Sinless perfectionism is an obsessively narcissistic goal anyway. Determine instead that you will be an example of an elder who knows how and when to repent, confess, and be restored to the mind of Christ. This reconciling spirit will stand you in better stead with the flock than an unblemished record, and it will make you approachable by those who have wounds and struggles. What is that old line from a Thornton Wilder play? "In love's service, only the wounded can serve!"

12. Call on the Sick. JAMES 5:14

This is not an optional part of your pastoral duty as an elder that can be "hired done" by professional pastors. If you don't know how to structure and conduct a simple encouragement call, ask your pastor to teach you; that's her job. Making these calls is yours! Congregational confidence in elder leadership rises in direct proportion to appreciation for the compassion and effectiveness of this simple ministry. If you want to know what you can do as an elder to improve the morale around your congregation–this is "job one." Many elders I know scribble personal notes from their own desks that acknowledge a member's troubled circumstance and provide a living reminder of the Lord's presence and love. Most Disciples congregations have long included homebound communion calls in their pastoral expectations of elders.

Many Disciples congregations are now experimenting with sacramental healing services and provide such prayer services, led by elders, who also offer communion and the biblical healing ritual of anointing with oil and the laying on of hands. These spiritual practices are no longer segmented to the charismatic or pentecostal sects; they have moved significantly into mainline practice, and they are enormously comforting to our flocks when led by those whose ego is not in the way and who understand that the Lord is the healer, not us. Practicing this kind of sacramental healing for the sick is one way for elders to manifest faith in the One who is mysteriously at work in the heart of all things.

13. Be Teachable and Teaching. Titus 1:9

Elders are eagerly engaged in a learner lifestyle, which is made up of small, positive learning habits. We have to be lifelong learners of the faith before we can ever hope to "pass it on." There is no substitute for this kind of commitment to and love of spiritual learning; otherwise, our opinions start to harden around the edges and calcify into "the way it has always been." If pastoral ministry to the sick is "job one" for elders, then "requirement one" is cultivating a teachable spirit within. Listening with a heart ready to obey and joyfully putting into practice those insights gained from scripture, prayer, and conversation are what eldering is all about. A person can learn most everything else needed about "doing what elders are supposed to do," but sincere teachability only comes when one chooses with Mary the "one thing [that] is needful," (Lk. 10:42, KJV). All the gifts of teaching that help us pass on the faith to the next generation flow out of our own moments of quiet devotion before the Lord. We lose our teachable spirit at our own peril!

14. Exercise Faithfulness. 2 Timothy 2:2

Most of God's kingdom work is done by people who have already put in a full day's work by the time they get to church. As leaders, those things we would not get around to do "just because we felt like it," we would graciously do because it is part of our communal understanding that we are Christ's body in the world: his (arthritic) hands, his (tired) feet, his (broken) heart. Representing his presence requires us to be present consistently, dependably, with a steady loyalty and a feisty determination to "hang in there" with one another, regardless of the circumstances.

This kind of faithfulness proclaims the gospel as effectively as any elaborate sermon. I have come to call this "the blessed sacrament of showing up." Eighty-eight percent of eldering is showing up and trusting the Spirit to teach you the rest!

3

The Elder and the Chalice

I recently visited Lindenwood Christian Church in Memphis, Tennessee. This is one of our large, old-yet-bold, cutting-edge congregations in the process of spiritual transformation under the pastoral guidance of Dr. C. Roy Stauffer. My imagination was captured by a piece of art that senior associate minister Owen Guy displayed in one of his famous hallway art galleries. Owen effectively engages all the mediums of art to dramatize the Christian message. This particular piece had been created in the church's woodshop and studio. The wooden shield featured the Disciples chalice with the Saint Andrew's cross. Streams of radiating light from the chalice were portrayed by variegated colors and grains of wood forming the background. As a woodworker, I was fascinated by this simple yet effective combination of multigrained woods forming a background for the chalice as the focal point of the carving.

As I studied this handiwork, I sensed my soul being drawn toward God through the artistic medium. It came to me, *Perhaps you need to just spend a few minutes allowing this piece of art to speak for itself.* As I quietly gave myself to a moment of meditation, an invitation came: *Why not allow this piece of art to function in your imagination as a kind of icon?* Icons have long been used in the history of the church as a simple window into the soul, whereby the spiritual heart forms a picture that, as we wait upon the Lord, creates a "way in" to the divine Presence via meditative imagination. As I allowed this image to form in my mind and shape my consciousness, I began to recognize in the contours of this chalice art some semblance of the flow of our work as elders in the life of the church.

An Image at the Heart of Disciples Eldership

The intersecting symbols of cup and cross that characterize the Disciples chalice convey a powerful image for understanding an elder's life. At the heart of Disciples eldership is a strong theology of both cross and cup.

Theology of the Cross

Elders never live far from the core meaning of the cross: He died for me. Although we may study scripture and theology for a lifetime and never fully fathom the depths of the atonement, we do understand this: When we stand beneath the cross and look up at Jesus' suffering love, we can never be the same again. We are eternally affected, and we rise from our knees renewed in our vows. Yes, in some way we will never fully understand yet seek always to honor, the sacrificial life, death, and resurrection of Christ is at the core of all we are and are about as elders of the body of Christ.

The cross is the principal transformative event in the salvation history of our world. John 3:16 so powerfully captures the essence of this impact. Elders are leaders who have chosen to live the cruciform life—that is, in conformity with the pattern of the cross. Elders embody, on a daily basis, the drama of their baptism: The old self is dead and buried with Christ, and the new self is raised up to walk in the power of Christ's resurrection life.

Effective elders have allowed the Holy Spirit to shape and form this baptismal formula into a living consciousness within. Effective elders passionately long to know this crucified and risen

Christ in an increasingly intimate way (Phil. 3:10). Although the church will always need scholars who help us delve into vast unexplored theological dimensions of the cross and keep its significance ever before us, the primary theologians of the cross must ever be elders whose practical everyday lives are the experiential application of the cross. Elders bring the song of the cross home to human hearts. Elders long to live in both the *shadow* ("Beneath the Cross of Jesus," *Chalice Hymnal,* no. 197) and *glory* ("In the Cross of Christ I Glory," *CH,* 207[1]) of the cross.

Theology of the Cup

As elders we may be inclined to discount and disconnect our own personal sufferings from the sufferings of Christ and not make the vital connection that heals, energizes, and empowers for service. Peter's epistle (1 Pet. 4:13–5:1) recognizes the link that blesses our own sufferings for the sake of Christ and sanctifies human spiritual leadership. Can you imagine what might happen if, instead of considering our experiences of suffering too unworthy and too embarrassing to even talk about, we made an offering of our sufferings to the Lord? Just as Christ relinquished his life in those final moments on the cross, so might we, moment by moment, release and offer up our struggles and sufferings to God. Then God, in God's own way, can mold and make of our broken lives whatever God chooses. Both resurrection and transformation are born of such intense spiritual yieldedness. Salvation itself is accomplished through the agency of such surrender. What if we practiced this vital connection in our prayer life?

In Philippians 3:10–11, Paul alluded to this vital connection between our sufferings and Christ's as the link to our most intimate knowledge of Christ. God's honest truth is this: The suffering that falls into our lives and we consider "most personal" and "strictly private" is in fact most universal. As we choose to use our own sufferings in the cause of Christ, we begin to "offer up" instead of "give up."

---

[1]All further references to hymns from *Chalice Hymnal* (St. Louis: Chalice Press, 1995) are identified by this abbreviation, *CH.*

This choice on our part makes all the difference in what we have to offer others we minister to within Christ's body. Ministering out of our own woundedness is different from bleeding all over others. As our own wounds are bound up and progressively healed by the Christ Spirit, we have access to the spiritual power of empathy.[2] Out of our own deep experiences of Christ's progressive healing, we are drawn to the sufferings of others and gladly offer a simple witness to the healing power of Christ's love. We discover that our gratitude for such astonishing grace at work in the heart of our soul becomes a powerful motivation to reach out and pour out our loving service for the least, the last, and the lost. In this respect, our service at the communion table each Sunday becomes a spiritual reenactment of what has been going on all week. Here is no empty ritual, hollow of the Holy! Here is exactly how elders embody our theology of the cup of Christ's sufferings, of which we all partake.

The Rhythm of a Cup Filled and Poured Out
Our Cup Is Filled

Life empties our cup. The demands and needs of life are so daily; we simply pour our lives into a multitude of commitments. Worries drain our energies, and work saps our strength. In order for spiritual leaders to have anything left to offer that is worthwhile, we need to learn how to feed our souls. One of the marks of a mature spirituality is the capacity to attend to our own souls before God in such a way that our cup is filled. Elders are able to feed themselves spiritually. Elders are more like mature eagles than like baby birds. Baby birds are always yapping and have to be fed constantly by someone else to keep them satisfied. Eagles know where food is found and how to secure it and feed themselves.

At least three things fill our cups as spiritual leaders. First is the worship of God. Nothing feeds the soul like spending time in the presence of God in praise and gratitude, living on the Easter

---

[2]On this topic, see Glen Boyd, *The A.R.T. of Agape Listening* (Sugarland, Tex.: Agape House Press, 1996).

side of the cross. If we are so distracted with serving on Sunday morning that we cannot personally enter into the spirit of worship, we might consider attending a second worship service each week where we can. Maybe Wednesday night or a small group can become our time for feeding the soul. We need to avail ourselves of a worship occasion *at least* each week. It's that important! Only our eager anticipation of the presence of God and our encounter with the holy can equip us to serve as elder. Everything else is window dressing.

Second, the overwhelming grace of God breaks in and overtakes us in the midst of daily life. Here the Holy Spirit refreshes, renews, and refills the energy we have emptied out in kingdom service. In accordance with the way Disciples interpret Acts 2:38, the Spirit's indwelling is continually abiding within as a gift actualized through our original baptismal experience. This indwelling power is outpoured and replenished in the ebb and flow of life in the Spirit. We simply respond to this grace by continually making room for the Spirit, by intentionally creating a welcoming heart.

Third, the habits and practices of our inner, devotional life before God express our intention to live in continual communion with the Holy One. From the human side, we develop certain habits of the heart that assist our search for the presence of God. To our constant blessing and amazement, God is faithful to God's promise and so gracious as to honor our intentions and join us at the tent of meeting (Ex. 40:34). For example, one way we attend the Presence is by reading scripture slowly and allowing it to form and reform us. Or we might raise an altar and make a temple for the Presence to dwell within through contemplation. Habits of the soul express our deepest desire to meet and be met by the living God. Traditional devotional disciplines may need some revising and refreshing in order to help cultivate our awareness of God, but my experience is this: While leadership is all grace, God expects me to receive this grace gratefully and to do so through receptivity to proven spiritual practices. As we faithfully attend our desire for God, God is so good as to make God's self known, which fills our cup.

For further reflections on how an elder may develop a discipline of spiritual practice that "fills the cup," see chapter 6.

Our Cup Is Poured Out

At its core, eldering among Disciples involves attending the powerful meanings present for us in the signs of the cup and the cross. The heart of our faith is found at the foot of the cross, where the salvation we were helpless to accomplish was accomplished for us through the gracious action of God in Jesus Christ. The cross as an historic event witnesses the work of reconciliation whereby God brought back together that which belongs together but is apart. That is, the longing of the human heart for God is united once again with the longing of God for communion with us. Our estrangements are decisively dealt with in the Christ moment. He bore our sorrows and sins in his body on the tree, and by his stripes we are healed. This is a forever fact, and we have the privilege of living it out in our daily lives. The application of Christ's atonement to our lives through soul-searching self-examination, prayers of confession, and the assurance of forgiveness make us "at-one" with the Holy and opens the way for communion between spirits human and Holy. As the healing of the purpose of our own life occurs, we are once again filled and prepared to serve as the heart and hands of Christ in the world.

The Disciples symbol of the Saint Andrew's cross speaks of the atoning work of Christ, who reconciles and redeems, transforming us into willing witnesses of God's healing power. We know the apostle Andrew was the witness who couldn't help himself; he had to tell the good news. Grace spilled out over the edges of his life, and his contagious enthusiasm for Christ was winsome and powerfully effective. May it be just so in our lives as well. The cup itself, filled to overflowing is spilled–spilled out in kingdom service. Graciousness is the sign of this sacrificial outpouring of our lives, both to God in praise and prayer, and to others in need. This is the deep core, the very heart and soul of the work of elders.

For further reflections on the pouring out of the elder's cup, see chapters 4, 5, and 7.

4

The Elder's Calling

Guiding Metaphors

Kedging the Anchor

I stumbled across the image of kedging the anchor through the creative writing of Len Sweet in his recent book *AquaChurch.*[1] It comes from navy life. Most landlubbers think harbor is the safest place for the ship to survive a storm. Because winds may drive a ship aground and allow damage to other boats, the harbor is often not the safest spot. When a storm is brewing, the captain orders the anchor crew to lift the anchor, place the chain on a dingy, and head straight out of the harbor, where a deeper, more secure place to anchor the ship may be found. Once the anchor is deeper out and more secure, the captain hauls the ship out to safety by kedging or pulling the ship out to safety on the anchor line. Picture the elders of the congregation as the anchor crew, who, risking danger to themselves in their little dingy, salt spray in their faces, are bravely responsible for securing the anchor in deeper but dangerous waters and kedging the ship to safety. This is a selfless and courageous task. Rearranging anchors while a storm is threatening is not a popular assignment, and is certainly not for the fainthearted! Our congregations get in trouble when

---

[1]Leonard Sweet, *AquaChurch* (Loveland, Colo.: Group Publishing, 1999).

the captain doesn't forecast the storm and call the anchor crew to task. Sometimes the crew is AWOL. There is a great deal one can gain from continuing to delve into this metaphor.

Getting Out of the Boat

John Ortberg works imaginatively with Peter's "walking on water" dilemma in his recent work *If You Want to Walk on Water, You Have to Get Out of the Boat.*[2] The driving force of this metaphor is the peaceful presence of a calm Christ who draws us out of the safety of the church basement to a high spiritual adventure beyond the realm of tried and true. We are living in times that call for something stronger than surrounding storms to order our existence. It is time to reach beyond the security of the four walls of First Christian Church. We are called to boldly risk reaching out to the least, the last, and the lost for the sake of the church's mission, with our hand in the hand of the man who stilled the waters. Our capacity for audacity needs exercising. Plenty of meditation material can be found here.

Museum or Mission Post?

Bill Easum, in one of his recent Beeson Institute seminars, first called my attention to the notion that our church buildings are being exceedingly well-preserved because we treat them as museums (look, but don't touch; don't use as a tool, just pass through and observe; primary resources allotted to preservation) instead of as mission posts on the frontier edge of a society that is increasingly hostile (not just indifferent) to Christianity. Suppose Easum is right and churches are again spiritual outposts. What does that make elders? How about missionaries to our own culture?

These three metaphors function in my thinking as icons when I am looking for ways to order the work of elders. As American Protestants, we are accustomed to dismissing icons as idols, but

---

[2]John Ortberg, *If You Want to Walk on Water, You Have to Get Out of the Boat* (Grand Rapids, Mich: Zondervan, 2001).

perhaps you are familiar with the way the Eastern Orthodox Church practices meditation by focusing on the image or icon as simply a "way in" to the Presence. By grace through faith amid mediation, the word picture opens up to become a door into the transforming reality of Christ's presence. Praying through and with these three mental pictures has drawn me through the knothole into a new dimension and new day in congregational life. I commend them to you, knowing your walk with God will carry you beyond the guidance of these metaphors to visions that inspire your elders' circle.

The Twin Challenges of Leadership and Companionship

If we as elders choose to take to heart our spiritual conformity to the cross and make it an actual way of life, a lifestyle—*Stand back!* We are just barely dipping our toes into the waters that the angel is stirring as we sit by the pool of Bethesda (Jn. 5:1–17). Serious challenges to our choice will arise all along the way in the major work areas of leadership and companionship.

Leadership

Being a Christlike leader in a businesslike church is never easy. Perhaps the place to begin is by simply confessing that we Disciples have become overly enamored, if not completely captured by, the corporate mentality of the culture in which we minister. Yes, we want to do things decently and in order, but consider the extent to which such conformity to a strictly business mentality has robbed the church of its spiritual power. Let's face it, Disciples in American culture are in nearly the same shape as Pope Leo IV, who showed Thomas Aquinas the vast treasures of the Vatican and commented slyly, "So you see, the church can no longer say with Saint Peter: 'Silver and gold have I none!'" Aquinas quickly replied, "Neither can the church say with Saint Peter: 'Rise up and walk!'"[3]

---

[3]G. Curtis Jones and Paul H. Jones, *500 Illustrations: Stories from Life for Preaching and Teaching* (Nashville: Abingdon Press, 1998).

Our vast wealth coupled with our passion for efficiency and orderliness need not be antithetical to spiritual vitality. However, to balance this tension, our churches need a strong elder leadership who are living out the cruciform life amidst the congregation.

What would cruciformity look like in church life? Look at the current winds of change blowing through church structure and administration in the American mainline Protestant churches as addressed by Bill Easum and Thomas Bandy. I do not subscribe to the theory of change for change's sake. Change is too costly, difficult, and painful to pull off in our local churches. Besides, there's too much opposition, which is exactly why so many leaders have decided "it's just not worth it." But change is not optional; it's inevitable. The only thing even more painful than change is becoming a dinosaur. Watching a congregation in the throes of a slow, agonizing, painful death while in a state of denial is the only thing more painful than change.

One example is our functional committee system. Many Disciples congregations practice a variation of this administrative style, which came into vogue during the golden age of mainline Protestantism. These structures are now collapsing under their own weight, yet we continue to prop the committee system up and hope it will run "one more year." I don't really think tinkering with the organizational structure will bring salvation to a sinking church, but I do think Thomas Bandy nailed it in his book *The Addicted Church*.[4] Our churches are addicted to a sick and self-perpetuating system that will only be broken by the courage of elders who will, with their pastors, seek God's vision for their congregation and boldly lead through whatever purgatory may be necessary to reestablish the congregation as a spiritual community on a mission from God! In his recent work, "From Mainline to Frontline,"[5] Dick Hamm plots the mainline church's

[4]Thomas Bandy, *Kicking Habits: Welcome Relief for Addicted Churches* (Nashville: Abingdon Press, 1997).

[5]Dick Hamm, "From Mainine to Frontline," *Lexington Theological Quarterly* 31, no. 1 (Spring 1996).

move from the sideline to the frontline of mission and service. If his optimism proves prophetic, it will be because the eldership is spiritually fit and prepared to speak up and step up into the gaps and gasps of congregations who insist, "But we've never done it that way before!" Pastors simply cannot pull off this kind of systemic change without teaming up with elders who have developed a high sensitivity to "what the Spirit is saying to the churches" (Rev. 2:29) and are not afraid to witness to their vision!

Companionship

This is the pastoral and caring aspect of eldership. First is the crying need for elders to simply be present when the church gathers. I call this "the blessed sacrament of showing up"–for weddings and funerals, for special occasions within church life, for moments that honor and appreciate others, when there is a need, and when it's time to clean up a mess. Elders themselves are rarely cognizant of their ministry of presence at such special services and gatherings, but members note our presence and are touched by it. Another very effective way of extending your ministry of presence for others is through notes and cards and phone calls. Dashing off a handwritten note from your desk at work may make some shut-in's day.

The ministry of companionship also embraces the practice of pastoring your pastor by recognizing his or her humanity and honoring that frailty without throwing stones or playing games that put them on the pedestal only to be knocked off later. Elders who know their pastors as real people with joys and struggles, with passions and problems, who need all the real help they can get, are invaluable. The willingness to work alongside the pastor as a colleague and trusted friend is often the unheralded difference between effective ministry and failure.

Elders who are willing to invest in an authentic relationship with their pastor may discover a kind of "holy spirit" role through intercession. Offering the insights and truths you gain through prayer on your pastor's behalf can be an enormous source of strength and blessing. You are yoked with your pastor in leadership and discipleship. So get acquainted, get real, and be an authentic part of each other's life! Be there for each other and live out your loyalty to God through loyalty to each other. Your faithfulness, even when you do not always agree, will earn you the right to say those difficult things that only elders can say to their pastors (and only pastors can say to their elders). Here's where humor helps.

The ordering of your work as an elder flows out of your life with God, both individually and corporately. In Acts 6 we get the impression that the spiritual leaders of the Jerusalem church centered their souls on prayer and serving the Word (Acts 6:4). On the personal level, this spiritual commitment may be expressed by an inner life of devotion and prayer congruent with an outer life of service and witness. On the corporate level, this calls for the formation of a core spiritual community within the congregation in which the faith is practiced, and the power of this resolve flows into community vision and mission as well as praise and worship. (See chapter 5.)

Four Key Roles

As elders intentionally cultivate an inner life centered on grace, our cup of spiritual insights, illuminations, and blessings fills up, and we are ready to pour out our energies in Christ's service through the daily life of eldering. Eldering is a lifestyle, a way of being and doing. Eldering can be an action verb as well as a noun. Effective eldering encompasses four primary dimensions of the work: encourager, mentor, shepherd, and servant.

1. Encourager

The congregation deserves and needs to know your mind, and not simply in matters of church politics, reasonable judgment, and wise discernment of disputes. Your congregation needs to know how you receive and pass on the simple daily spiritual encouragements that keep us all plugging away in kingdom service when times get tough. Your personal expressions of faith, hope, and love will win the day and hearts of the congregation. They regularly need to hear your willing witness. Whether you express them publicly in table prayer, occasions of public testimony, or perhaps in personal conversation, your words of encouragement backed up by your example pack a strong spiritual impact in the life of the congregation. Your words and inspirational deeds touch the congregation at the deepest level of its being and nourish the congregation's will to be about its work. The fruit of your walk with God becomes transparent to others as you practice optimism and hope. Elders are tonic people, not toxic people. Elders are fun people to be around because they are generally (ok, we all have occasional bad days) a blessing and uplifting strength to others—even when they are not trying. People have placed their confidence in you and your consistent, faithful "good word." Spiritual connectivity is no casual thing to be treated lightly; it is an honorable trust. The congregation wants you to exhort, to rekindle the flame, to stir up the neglected spiritual gifts within, to lift and laugh and love and remind and graciously help refocus. This spiritual connectivity is a sacred responsibility that also bears with it the power to fulfill this need. As you step up to this task, the energy to accomplish it may surprise you.

2. Mentor

Many elders possess the spiritual gifts for teaching and preaching, and they need to be heard from on significant occasions. Such gifts may be celebrated and elevated, supported and coached by their pastors. With regard to teaching gifts, we need to reinvent the old "pastor's class" model of baptismal instruction, whereby children in the fourth grade and older are invited to study for a few weeks before Easter. This approach needs to give way to a creative teaching/mentoring partnership. Let the class be led by elder-pastor teams. As churches learn to include elders in this mentoring process, a new bond of spiritual connection and friendship is forged between the generations. Elders have the privilege of getting to know and participate with young people at this critical juncture in the young persons' spiritual lives.

Volunteer to teach vacation Bible school, Sunday school, and special children/youth events. Kids need to hear from their elders and connect with you on a personal level. Enough good things can't be said about the power of the personal example of our Disciples elders. When elders are placed in proximity with our young learners, it consistently seems to draw out something healthy and positive for all ages! An intangible spiritual blessing is passed on, along with the content of the class or learning situation. Our churches need strong, straightforward moral leadership by leaders who are patient, gracious, and accepting while clear and firm. We cannot afford to remain silent about the subtle, corrosive power of sin to the soul while loving and mentoring. A new balance must be struck, and elders can do this.

Gentle, positive power for good wins the day. While this is an intangible dimension of leadership, it is one that consistently helps open the door for good things to happen. Elder's attitudes help set the corporate atmosphere that creates a positive climate for worship and growth. Our churches are desperate for this sense of blessing.

3. Shepherd

Tending the flock is not the job you hire the pastor to do. It is a lifelong lifestyle to which elders are called as partners with pastors. Breaking this "hire-it-done" mentality means breaking out of church meetings and getting out there–being where the sheep actually are. Ballgames, civic events, grocery shopping, the daily tasks of life can be moments of ministry. Our flocks cannot be guided to pastures green unless we are out in the fields, stirring among them, circulating. Connecting, checking in on (which feels a lot different from checking up on), remembering anniversaries and birthdays, stopping to speak, acknowledging joys and struggles and special occasions, expressing your sensitivity to known needs–these are all shepherding expressions.

This is the ministry of touching in, as elders trust the ever-present Christ within to be the Good Shepherd in each moment and each contact. It need not always be a two-hour conversation on the sidewalk outside the supermarket, but active listening skills let people know you care about what is going on with them. Shepherding is not always feeling called on (or put upon) to solve people's problems, but it is being the human bridge for them to the Great Shepherd of our souls. Your caring contact with them helps them make the spiritual connection they need to sustain their souls. Being with people on all sorts of occasions helps them identify with your very humanness, even as you guide or move them along to new experiences of spiritual growth to which God may be calling.

The quality and quantity of your caring as an elder show up in odd places. For instance, vitality in a congregation's worship is often a strong indication that elders are shepherding and that folks feel cared for. If the daily needs of the congregation are being attended to through intercessory prayer as well as by effective elders who are pastoring the people, a joyful sense of spiritual expectation carries into worship life. This is one concrete expression of the elder's "holy spirit" role as John 14 portrays it. Elders come alongside to comfort, clarify, encourage, and commend. It's the ministry of "being there." The pastoral attitude that best carries this grace is a transparent willingness to be who we are before God before others.

4. Servant

Not unlike the early apostles who served the Word and attended the corporate prayer life of the congregation (Acts 6:4), the elders' primary service is Godward! We serve the Eternal One in praise and adoration by constantly touching into that place where the life of God is lived—in us, among us, and beyond us in the eternal realm. To borrow a metaphor from Revelation 5:14, the elders' eternal work is to join the everlasting song around the throne of God, praising and glorifying God forever. In John's vision, it is the elders' work to lay their crowns and prizes (trophies and tributes gleaned from a lifetime of service) before the One who alone is worthy.

The antithesis of this humble servant ministry as elders is the way we sometimes play the elder brother in the prodigal son story. Grumbling to the father, begrudging other sinners their moments in the sun of repentance, not appreciating the pain and suffering it takes to drive a soul to its knees, not honoring the sincerity of others, and grouching about the grace of God are all attitudes that do not exactly embody the heart of God. In contrast with the glorious, eternal work of elders, we confess the infernal work of elders as well. Namely, instead of casting crowns, we cast aspersions. Let's face it, sometimes we are quicker with mocking wit, criticism, and cynicism than we are with singing the Lamb's song. Aspersions cast by leaders lay on a burden instead of helping others lay down a burden. Aspersions are attitudes that weigh down and slow down souls from making spiritual progress. Aspersions are accusations that cut the soul to the quick. At another level, aspersions are a negative spiritual dynamic attributed to the evil one, who is the accuser of the Christian conscience (Rev. 12:10). Aspersions add no lift, verve, and nerve to a congregation who desperately needs spiritual momentum. Congregations are like an old Boeing 747 rumbling down the runway trying to gather up momentum for liftoff; congregations do not need drag at this point. Aspersions are a drag; aspirations are a lift. Servant leaders lend lift to the congregation's momentum, not drag.

A positive way to talk about servant leadership is the footwashing scene in John 13. Servant leaders willingly set aside the garments that symbolize their own rights, privileges, and entitlements. Elders who give themselves unselfishly to the needs of others, as a servant of the servants of Christ, are rare. Our churches need elders who will take up the towel and wash feet. Humble service in the church means studying the fine print at the bottom of your elder ordination certificate: "whatever it takes to get the job done" or "and all such duties as may be assigned." If weeds in the prayer garden need pulling, pull! Elders are

Christ's servants of the servants of God. The higher our office in the church, the more people we carry in love. This is not to place the total burden for congregational life in the elders' circle. The yoke is shared with deacons, who are the worker bees of any congregation. Members who serve unselfishly out of their spiritual giftedness share servant tasks. Ordained pastors use their gifts to preach, teach, and equip servants for their ministries. Elders help form creative partnerships where we are linked as "yokefellows" with Christ, all pulling in the same direction!

It is amazing what can be accomplished for the kingdom cause when you have a circle of elders who don't really care who gets the credit and are regularly honoring and appreciating and uplifting all those who fulfill servant roles. Every time you catch somebody doing something right around the congregation, feel free to tell them all about it! Elders who eagerly and unselfishly serve for the glory of God are themselves the hidden glory of their congregations. If you are looking for ways to hone in on this concept, Robert Greenleaf's books *Servant Leadership* and *Servant Leadership in Church Settings* provide practical help. This Quaker clarifies the spirit of servant leadership as no one else currently writing in the field.

Twelve Key Areas of Responsibility

Shifting the organizational culture within a congregation in a positive way in order to "raise the bar" of expectation for elder work is no easy task, and there is no single way of achieving this shift. One positive way to change the expectation is by developing a proactive stance that goes beyond "here are the rules, now get with the program!" We might address this by stating positively what the elders are "in charge of" in congregational life.

1. The Atmosphere of the Congregation

Elders help set, shape, mold, and model the kinds of attitudes that create the climate for an atmosphere of wholesome fun, enjoying one another's company, treatment of one another in loving grace, creative partnership, hopeful anticipation, faithful expectation, and trustful permission-giving with regard to "new things." The tone of appreciation and praise for blessings and graces is the elders' work too! Something as fragile yet critical to well-being as "atmosphere" requires well-grounded and well-maintained trust within the elders. Constant watchfulness is the work of the shepherd.

2. The Pastoral Care of the Congregation

Of course, pastors will call and do their part in the care and feeding of the flock, but when all is said and done, more needs to be said and done by the elders. Sadly, most congregations have "hired" all their care professionally done and robbed one another of the joy of simply being there and caring for one another in the name of Christ. Perhaps it is time to recapture the spirit of the early church, which discerned that the apostles should focus their ministry on the Word and prayer, and oversee but not do (hands-on) all the care by themselves. Support, encourage, train, and guide? Absolutely! Participate? Yes, by all means. But be the hired hand? No. I would agree with Kenneth Callahan that there is a critical place for elder visitation, contact through notes and phone calls, and loving acknowledgement of people's needs in our Disciples churches. The elder's care directly affects morale.

3. Boundary Setting

Through a process of group discernment, the elders are responsible for the setting of healthy limits and boundaries on those behaviors or attitudes that are deemed inappropriate, out-of-bounds, detrimental, and even downright dangerous and destructive, both individually and to the community. If it is "not good for the body" and is tearing at the fabric of unity, it must be dealt with, and the elders are the proper group to exercise pastoral authority. They are likewise in charge of finding gracious yet firm and loving ways of communicating these communal limits of appropriate behavior and attitude to those who need this loving limit set forth for them as a solid, unwavering, and dependable boundary to bounce up against in dealing with their own "out-of-control" situation. This is the beginning place for a new definition of the old term "spiritual accountability."

4. Example Setting

Elders bear the weight of helping others—making it easier to believe in the Christian way of life by the grace with which they live it out. They need to do all they can within their collective power to help one another become the best examples of excellence in practical wisdom for Christian living that are available in the congregation. This means leading the way in appreciating the positive examples of faith among the congregation and honoring them. It includes a gracious benediction on the elderly, whose lifetime of service calls for recognition for the sake of example. Being the living Christ for one another is the elder's calling.

5. Spiritual Expectation

Elders are in charge of creating—by the power of their own faith, intercessions, and verbal witness—a powerful sense of expectation that something good and of God is just on the verge of happening in our worship service this morning (or evening). Living on tiptoe, they hold their breath in joyful expectation that the Spirit of the Holy is already breaking in on the worship prepared by spirits human, and is creating a new day. They come to church or a special meeting with the clear, solid, thankful attitude that says: "I can't wait to see what God is up to next, and I definitely want to be in on that blessing!" Elders are either helping this grace unfold or are part of the conspiracy that keeps it from happening.

6. Living by Faith

Because we Disciples are, by nature or nurture, most comfortable with all things reasonable, logical, and rational, we sometimes live by sight instead of faith. Whenever the congregation has fallen into the trap of only aiming at and achieving goals or dreams that are already within sight or reasonable reach, it is time for the elders to climb on out on the limb with the ministers. (How's that for a big assumption?) Seriously, though, whatever happened to the later part of Acts 2? The part about "your young people shall see visions and your old people dream dreams"? Elders are in charge of dreaming big dreams for God, or at the very least honoring those among the congregation who do!

7. Companioning

Elders are in charge of playing a beautiful "holy spirit" role within the congregation by quietly coming alongside those who are hurting and in need or trouble. It is your privilege to support, encourage, and offer intercession. This may not necessarily include the offering of unsolicited advice. It is more the blessed ministry of "being there." If you were to ask the congregation what they most need from their spiritual leaders, this would be it. However, don't take my word for it; check it out in your own experience.

8. Welcoming

Elders are in the constant role of hosting, greeting, welcoming, and making comfortable the incessant parade of people who darken the doors. Here's the test for hospitality: When someone you don't know appears on your radar screen, what do you do? Don't wait for someone else who's "scheduled to be the official greeter" to step up. In this moment of transcendental hesitation, all is lost! Elders do not hang back and whisper, "Who is that in the blue shirt?" They are always among the very first persons to stick out their hands and smile and introduce themselves (hoping to goodness that the person in the blue shirt says his or her name so you can catch it this time!) Elders preside, not only symbolically at the Lord's table but also over every table in the fellowship hall, playing host, because it is to this purpose we were called and ordained. Elders embody the warm and welcoming spirit of the Gracious Host. Commit Romans 15:7 to memory; it will serve better than any Miss Manners guide.

9. Mentoring

Elders can multiply the hands and hearts who are actually doing the work of Christ by giving permission, coaching, and cheerleading others. This is a kind of Elijah role to the younger Elisha. Get comfortable casting the mantle of your leadership over younger shoulders. Learn how to use the Socratic method (and Jesus method too) of one-on-one teaching–asking questions to draw out those who want to learn. Elders still possess the personal power to raise up a new generation of leaders who will witness the gospel. Note: Your mentorees will not witness the gospel your way. Get used to this and get over it. However, this is not to say you should roll over and offer them no critique along with your encouragement. If you teach them to honor the spirit of faithfulness that transcends all cultural forms, they will pass the faith on and you will be able to recognize it and rejoice.

10. Focus Outward

Despite the pastor's brilliantly inspired sermons about "the need for us to rise up and become a Great Commission congregation," it is the elders who will hold a secret meeting in their collective heart-of-hearts and elect to make this critical decision: Will we be a mission post or a museum? By that I mean: "As the head is turned, the body will follow." No amount of pastoral persuasion, however clever, will ever convince a congregation that has grown comfortable shuffling deck chairs on the decks of the Titanic to turn outward *until* the elders, as the spiritual head, have turned the body in this outwardly focused direction. Otherwise the congregation may remain a lovely place of worship, but never quite actualize its true potential as an outpost, a mission station. If the elders can't see it, the congregation will never be it!

11. Collegial Support

The elders really bear a community responsibility to maintain their own corporate spiritual life as a body of leaders committed to the kingdom. The pastors and key elders are charged with this concern. In addition, elders bear the weight of sustaining their own individual spiritual lives through practicing those practices that enhance their presence for God. In order for elders to maintain a servant leader's lifestyle, they will need retreats and a variety of renewal experiences at regular intervals, designed and led by those who are nurturing and guiding the specific vision of your congregation. Here it is critical that the vision of your church's mission be uplifted in a fresh way so that some facet of this vision catches a gleam of light and reflects new radiance into the hearts of those at the heart of the work. Some such inspirational occasion should occur at least every six months. Uplifting the vision and reigniting the mission might also be linked with some very practical devotional help—perhaps a "how-to" session that explores a particular spiritual practice that is fascinating but unfamiliar. It may be helpful to vary the menu and format of these gatherings. One time the form may be a traditional retreat; another time it might be an evening of worship in a neighboring congregation. Another such occasion might be a quiet day devoted to prayer. I marvel how much some groups are able to accomplish over a Saturday morning breakfast that lasts about two hours and ends with prayer circle and renewed commitment. We do not just make the decision once to become an elder; we make it over and over again, day by day and retreat by retreat. We travel on this spiritual journey mile-marker by mile-marker, noting joys, setbacks, and side roads.

12. Discernment

Faithfully interpreting and embodying the ancient faith for a postmodern culture require creating a community within the congregational community in which a process of ongoing spiritual discernment can take place in an atmosphere of prayer, worship, the practicing of the practices, and conversation that is full of faithful trust in one another and in God's grace. In this age, our congregations confront a whole host of issues, concerns, problems, and situations that simply will not yield themselves to solutions through the kind of process we have created in our administrative board meetings where Roberts rules. We need the flexibility of a prayer-filled atmosphere where the Spirit rules. I have come to think of the elders' circle as just such a place, where an almost "Quaker-style" discernment process takes place, and we are able to listen to what the Spirit is saying to the church in such a way that we discover how to embody that truth in the congregation's worship life and witness.

5

The Elders' Circle

The ordering of your work as an elder flows out of your life with God, both individually and corporately. In Acts 6, we get the impression that the spiritual leaders of the Jerusalem church centered their souls on prayer and serving the Word (Acts 6:4). On the personal level, this spiritual commitment may be expressed by an inner life of devotion and prayer congruent with an outer life of witness and service, utilizing spiritual giftedness. On the corporate level, this calls for the formation of a core spiritual community within the congregation where the faith is practiced, and the power of this resolve flows into community vision and mission as well as praise and worship.

The Personal Level: Serving out of Your Spiritual Giftedness

How many times have we recruited warm bodies to fill program slots instead of inviting and inspiring leaders to search out their spiritual gifts and serve ministries out of their gift-strengths, as they envision God calling them?

Spiritual gifts are those special abilities with which believers are born and born again. The gift of the Holy Spirit and the spiritual gifts are given at the time of our baptism and abide with us as reflections of God's image within, until we discover them. Gifts can be brought to life by the indwelling Holy Spirit to build up the body of Christ and fulfill the unique destiny God has placed in each of our hearts. So sanctification, our continued growth toward the fullness of Christ, is one purpose the gifts serve, and edification, the building up of Christ's body, is the other purpose. The key to understanding our gifts as elders is to recognize that the gifts are not about us—designed and displayed to make us look good. The point is servanthood, in the great servant leader spirit of Jesus. He offered his gifts at the intersection where the world's great need and his own deep joy met, and the results were stunning for the kingdom of God.

One major preventative measure against spiritual burnout is discovering and serving out of our spiritual gifts. This means we have to become well informed about the subject. If you are squeamish about borrowing ideas from evangelicals (some Disciples are, you know), just relax. The Episcopalians have been working on the spiritual gift inventory concept for twenty years. Presbyterians and Methodists have gotten on board. Disciples church growth consultant Judy Turner's original inventory work was adapted and revised by a team of lay-trainers from First Christian Church (Frankfort, Kentucky) and is available free in short form or for $5 in full SHAPE booklet form. Materials that Disciples congregations are currently using are easily available and readily adaptable, so any elders' circle can begin with a thorough study and accounting of their individual and collective spiritual gifts. Until elders are knowledgeable of their own souls' giftedness and begin, through study and prayer, to discover the God-given power that flows out of these gifts, our churches will have a tough time with the revitalization process. So elders must start ordering their work in that area, namely, in their spiritual gifts.

The Corporate Level: Forming a Core Community of Practice

One effective way to practice this ordering of the elder's work is through implementing the concept of the elders' circle. I have developed and field-tested this idea in three congregations over thirty years and still find that, beyond worship, this is the single most critical spiritual engagement on my calendar. It involves a weekly one-hour gathering of all the elders for prayer, learning, and encouragement. Let me describe how it works.

1. The elders' circle meets one hour per week.

Making the time convenient when folks are at church anyway helps build the critical mass and habitual dimensions of this gathering. For instance, Wednesday nights before the fellowship dinner or Sunday morning early, before any services begin works well. The agreed-upon time needs to average more than 75 percent attendance to be effective. Surrendering an hour each week to be an elder in prayer, community, and spiritual agreement with other elders is the bedrock spiritual discipline.

2. The session always begins and ends on time, convened by the chair of elders.

This is a lay-led, lay-driven group convened by its own elected leader, who keeps the meeting on track with its agreed purpose. The chair may need to referee (blow the whistle and call fouls) at times, but simply guides the process and shepherds the group in a friendly way to keep it faithful to its purpose: practicing the faith.

3. The meeting format develops its own rhythm and becomes almost a ritual.

The format includes: five-minute devotion and prayer led by an elder, with responsibility passed around circle; ten-minute limited discussion of known pastoral needs and calling assignments; thirty-minute teaching time with pastor; fifteen-minute sentence prayer around the circle, holding hands.

4. The conversation remains focused.

This means no church business allowed, nor will chitchat co-opt the agenda either. Although there may be many confabs about church board matters and business operations before and after the gathering, the purpose of this gathering will be honored. This is not a "mini board meeting." Certainly, fellowship and personal visiting or sharing and catching up helps bond the group, but the agreement is that we will hold one another accountable by naming what is going on if we are off course. Any elder who has a crisis may bid for time and ask for help and prayer; otherwise, the agreed agenda rules.

5. Openheartedness prevails.

We want to build an atmosphere in which it is comfortable to be who you are before God and before the other elders of this circle. This calls for straight-up honesty that tells the truth in love yet builds a spirit of camaraderie through sharing joys and sorrows. If we expect to develop a warm and welcoming congregation, we have to model this spiritual expectation over time. Elders' souls are molded and shaped by sharing life together in core community. This molds a cohesive, positive, consensual spiritual force in the heart of the congregation.

6. Simple disciplines are practiced faithfully.

As we each "get a life" with God, through prayer and companionship with the Spirit, we also shape a common foundation on which our shared life may be built. We begin to open, disclose, and share this inner life with one another. A community forms that creates a new norm. Here it is acceptable to risk and share personal faith, explore deep convictions, confess areas where help is needed (even if not always appreciated), and express loving support of one another in ministry. Elders begin to elder one another and to receive eldering as well. Eldering becomes an active verb as well as a noun.

7. Spiritual enthusiasm builds momentum.

When eldering energy spills out over the edges of this circle and into the congregation, good things begin happening. Out of the experience of being eldered, elders learn effective ways to practice the ancient art of soul care and shepherding out in the congregation. Nothing raises morale and builds momentum for mission like a well-cared-for congregation.

8. A spiritual consensus emerges.

Four simple disciplines help keep the elders' circle on track: (a) Attending weekly meetings regularly unless out of town. (b) Maintaining strict confidentiality on all pastoral matters. Specifically, this means the conversation remains in the room and is not shared with spouses when we leave. (c) Willingness to step up to and own the spiritual authority and spiritual responsibility of the office of an elder. (d) Maintaining a willingness to ask for prayer.

9. Teaching stimulates spiritual growth.

Teaching topics led by the pastor may include questions and shared research around doctrines, current trends in American church life, sharpening conflict management skills, techniques in visitation, help in composing table prayers, dealing with matters of confidentiality, updates on Disciples church news nationally and regionally, pastoral care for persons with AIDS, how to make a twelve-step program referral, dealing with burnout, personal growth through tithing, principles of living wills or advanced directives, pastoral guidelines for remarriage, biblical background papers on research that might inform the eventual formation of congregational policy, clinical help with pastoral problems that might arise out of elder visitation, how to come alongside and encourage a person, how to support family members in the Alzheimer's process, what to say to a friend in grief, restoring a relationship through forgiveness, how to develop a deeper sense of discernment about God's will, studying famous sermons, digesting devotional classics, critical analysis for problem areas of church life, discernment about how to faithfully live out our core vision and values as a people, developing moral character through the fruits of the Spirit, learning how to do damage control with out-of-control personalities or situations, how to balance the priorities before trying to balance the budget, or last but not least, what elders can learn from famous prayers for composing their own, good old exegetical Bible study.

Serving up a spiritual teaching menu that includes a wide variety—breadth and depth, simple and complex, fun and heavy, intellectual engagement and emotional connection—appears to be the key to stimulating spiritual growth. Once the group process of a circle of elders begins to jell, and the gathering experiences some convergences, it is tempting to try to change the format. Anything more than this seems to engender organizational chaos, while anything less endangers our care of one another's souls.

Some elders may argue that with so many church meetings going on, why add one more? And a weekly one at that? It is because this is *the core* spiritual leadership gathering of the week. This is the one out of which all others are ordered. I like to say the reason Paul appointed elders as the "leaders on the ground" in every place his missionary journey carried him is that elders are God's heart. The spiritual essence of the heart of God is manifest in each group of elders. It matters to the spiritual health and overall well-being of the congregation how this circle chooses to discern the Presence! Weekly meetings are what it takes to sustain critical mass around vision, mission, and momentum over the long haul. Anything less produces fizzle where sizzle is needed.

The Personal and Corporate: A Summary of Expectations

The following statements sum up the expectations the elders develop toward themselves and one another in their time within and beyond the elders' circle.

1. Elders are expected to show up in the conference room every Wednesday from 5 to 6 p.m., unless the weekly meeting of the elders' circle is cancelled in advance.
2. Elders are invited to open their hearts before God and one another and set a tone in this gathering for loving trust and candor.

3. Elders are asked to become informed about issues that affect our corporate life and guide the formation of the congregational consensus.

4. Elders need to take the initiative and break through barriers of noncommunication, inertia, and passive-aggressive behavior to establish lines of communication and connection within the total life of the congregation. They are expected to be proactive!

5. Elders are expected to do their homework and come prepared to ask questions, discuss, and contribute to the conversation by active participation.

6. Elders accept as necessary those daily spiritual practices that sustain their life with God, and they are willing to witness to the faith, strength, and joy that come through this devotion.

7. Elders are expected to keep their own lives in order under God and to live an exemplary, Christ-reflecting life, recognizing that there is no such thing as perfection, only forgiveness.

8. Elders are encouraged to lean into the future, to be the ones who are dreaming dreams and seeing visions of God's unfolding purpose in the midst of our corporate life together.

9. Elders are encouraged to take their stewardship seriously and practice proportional giving toward the biblical benchmark of tithing (as a floor not a ceiling!).

10. Elders are required to maintain confidentiality (defined as: it stays in the room when we leave) and accountability (which means if we don't, we get called on it) to one another on pastorally sensitive matters where people's reputations are at stake.

11. Elders are asked to stand shoulder to shoulder with the pastoral staff in support, encouragement, and candor with love.

12. Elders are expected to be involved in the mentoring ministry by molding, shaping, encouraging, uplifting, and often in a quiet way—inspiring!

13. Elders are scheduled for communion prayers in worship services and requested to discipline their prayers by the guidelines offered in Peter Morgan's book.[1]

14. Elders are invited to operate out of the strengths of their spiritual gifts. This may on occasion require that we take on tasks that simply need to be done and no one else is doing them. At such times we are challenged to read the fine print: "such duties as may be needed!" Elders know how to "step up to the plate" and do so well!

15. Elders are encouraged to set the tone in meetings that turn negative and to actually get on the grapevine when necessary to counteract gossip. Elders are in charge of the spiritual atmosphere of the congregation and patiently trace rumors to their source and set the record straight, challenging and correcting as needed.

---

[1]Peter M. Morgan, *Disciples Eldership: A Quest for Identity and Ministry* (St. Louis: Christian Board of Publication, 1993).

6

Sustaining the Work of an Elder

As elders we cannot meet the challenge of leadership and companionship with an empty cup! One elder I know always slips into the sanctuary well before folks start filling the pews and double-checks the communion trays to make certain the cups are full. (That's because one Sunday she lifted the lid just before her communion prayer and beheld to her horror, the trays were utterly empty.) She then pauses for a moment of quiet prayer that helps focus her soul on this Sunday's worship, remembering all those who will play key roles in the service and all who will fill the pews. No wonder her prayers always seem to be "right on target" and carry her congregation into the Presence with a certain freshness and vitality!

I suppose every elder knows that sinking feeling of heartsick panic when the bulletin declares, "You're up this Sunday," but you're feeling "way off," oddly out of sync and out of sorts. As we examine the reasons behind this feeling of not being prepared, it may be that we have run around all week, attending to everything and everyone else, but neglecting our own soul! We have been running around with our gas tank on "E," assuming it means "Enough," but it actually reads "Empty!" Our presiding over the table becomes a moment of truth, as our table prayer falls flat. Even if it is flawlessly executed, we know that haunting sense of hollowness as the prayer we audibly form fails to uplift and energize even us. Sometimes our prayer feels empty because so are we. Now don't try to argue that "God sovereignly uses our failures, His wonders to perform." Let's just 'fess up on the freewill side of the equation! Our failure to attend those spiritual practices that would fill our cup has a way of finally catching up with us. Here's where we pause to lift up our empty lives to life's Giver and Sustainer, singing, "Fill my cup, Lord." Simply put: We cannot run around eldering with an empty cup while being in charge of filling everyone else's.

I have wondered if our Disciples tendency to overvalue church activity and undervalue the reflective side of our faith may be related to the way we have been formed spiritually. American mainline Protestant Christianity, particularly as currently practiced by Disciples, is overloaded on the rational and activistic side of the equation while we are typically undeveloped on the quietistic, devotional aspect of life with God.

There are strong historical reasons for this lack of balance. Scholars such as Joe Driscoll, Bill Paulsell, and Newell Williams have traced these traditions to their roots. Their work thoroughly documents our failure to appreciate the need for balance in the realms of intellect, emotion, and inspiration. As Disciples we tend to overvalue the rational and intellectual approach to faith. During the critical times, when Disciples spirituality was being formed, this was a needed corrective to an insipid revivalism that had long lost its own heart and fallen into heavy-duty dependence on revivalist techniques. As a necessary corrective, Disciples were taught by their spiritual leaders to notice and highly prize the rational and intellectual approach to faith.

All well and good—for that time and season. Indeed this is our heritage through the Campbell side of the Restoration Movement. Do a meditative study of William Paulsell's sketch of the warm and emotive side of Alexander Campbell's faith in his excellent book, *Disciples at Prayer*.[1] You may be amazed at the ardor and devotion with which Campbell approached prayer and his personal spiritual life. You don't have to read between these lines to realize that the chief proponent of our esteemed Disciples intellectual tradition anchored his intellect on a foundation of devotion, adoration, and a rich prayer life. Campbell's enormous mental energy and intellectual curiosity were born out of deeply entrenched habits that became for him a way of life that incorporated the ancient and daily practice of prayer and devotion. Closer examination reveals the equation was more carefully balanced than we have been led to believe. Perhaps it is time to address this balance.

With regard to the need for spiritual leaders to find ways to fill their cups, one of Fred Craddock's sermon illustrations made a lasting impression on me. Fred recalls visiting in the hospital when suddenly he was accosted, quizzed as to his identity as "a preacher," and summarily kidnapped. To his famous befuddlement, Fred was whisked out of the hallway by anxious family members who ushered him to the bedside of a woman whom he did not know. She was suffering a traumatic health crisis, had just been given "bad news," and was preparing herself for critical surgery. As they talked, Fred looked around the room, hoping to gain some insight into the measure of spiritual resources she might have gathered around her to comfort her soul in this decisive battle for her life. All he saw was a stack of movie magazines and tabloids such as those found at the grocery store checkout. He shook his head in wonderment. There wasn't enough spiritual oomph in that whole stack to save her soul, let alone carry her through a tough surgery.

Fred's point is well taken, elders. Do your personal reading habits help sustain your soul as an elder? Is there enough spiritual strength in the stack to save and sustain your soul? We may need to reevaluate the strength of our reading material and take on provisions that will fortify us with more substance for difficult

---

[1]William O. Paulsell, *Disciples at Prayer* (St. Louis: Chalice Press, 1995).

days. Reading and study are two primary ways our spirits are formed and informed. Stephanie Paulsell's recent lecture at Lexington Seminary speaks to the excellence of this spiritual discipline.[2]

So how can we learn to draw water from the deep wells of salvation? We will need the cup of trust and surrender.

1. *Trust.* Let's develop a simple, childlike confidence in the sheer grace of God that is ministered to us in all the ways we so desperately need it. Our focus is to remain open and gratefully receive what God so graciously gives. Here we practice a theology of grace that empowers us to live in humble appreciation for the blessing that constantly surrounds us, and in thanksgiving that God, who invented "on-time" manufacturing, will indeed provide what we need just when we need it most. We learn to live our way into a trust that God will supply our needs (Eph. 3:16; Phil. 4:19). Elders are entrusted to hold in trust the very power of God. Elders enjoy the bounteous feast of God (Ex. 18:12), and offer the blessing of God's feast to others as well. As stewards of the mysteries of God (1 Pet. 4:10), "we have this treasure in clay jars, so that it may be made clear that this extraordinary power belongs to God and does not come from us" (2 Cor. 4:7).

2. *Surrender.* Here we seek to honor the example of Christ, who offered up his life and energy to God for a purpose beyond his own. Surrender and obedience are not popular concepts in our culture, but to cultivate the mind of Christ through these practices, we need to learn all we can about this matter. We do this by putting into practice the most basic practices of our faith.

Spiritual Practices

Seeking a spirituality that would sustain elders' souls in the rigors of parish life turns most Disciples in many directions for help. We are great ecumenical borrowers. We beg, borrow, and steal anything from Willow Creek to Battle Creek, from Amy Grant to Taizé. Some of us quite comfortably turn toward the "high church" traditions and find a healing balm in the language

---

[2]Stephanie Paulsell, *Lexington Theological Quarterly* 36, no. 3 (Fall 2001).

of liturgy and rituals, retreats and silence, with the mystical Christ as our solace. Others of us just as naturally turn toward evangelical roots as a way to recover, through the discipline of a morning watch or devotional quiet time, a fresh focus on Jesus and scripture in our own experience of the heart.

For Disciples, the question "But is it Disciple?" is subordinate to the question "Does it work?" Practicality is very Disciple! Ours is a pragmatic approach to spirituality, based experientially on whether a given practice provides some felt sense of a way whereby we find ourselves ushered into the Presence.

Instead of assuming we need another seminar or workshop before we can become the type of spiritual "super-elder" we have always longed to be, why not begin simply walking the time-honored paths that lead to transformational faith? While we need the occasional encouragements and reminders of workshops, the spirituality of elders is an "inside job" anyway.

Spiritual disciplines are the "habits of soul" we develop on a daily basis that open us to the presence of God. They provide "ways in" or "paths of practice." This accent helps us recall that Christianity is essentially a way of life, with Jesus as the Way. Spirituality is a path we walk with the living Christ toward the union of our souls with God.

It takes time, patience, and grace to walk the path toward God. Early on, we may get caught up in concerns of technique or methodology. We fret about whether we are "doing it right." Eventually we learn that even this question focuses too much attention on the anxious ego trying to master a technique or control an outcome. Gradually we walk the path with less distraction, devoting ourselves to God for whatever God might do (or not do) with us. The paths that seem to lead us consistently into the Presence become well worn and much beloved.

Research into current practices of Christian spirituality yields exciting insights into dozens of specific ways we can walk moment by moment with Christ. For psychological reasons footnoted here but not fully developed, our learning style and personality type may have major impact on which practices we as elders find most helpful in assisting our search for the presence of God. For instance, extroverted personalities may be naturally drawn to certain forms of prayer and find others quite tedious. (You may learn more about this in *Please Understand Me.*[3])

Out of the myriad ways to practice the presence of God in our lives, I have selected nine practices that Disciples elders in retreats and workshops seem to find most helpful. For each of the nine practices, I offer a brief description, some words of instruction to help launch and guide you on the path, and some questions to prompt journal reflection. The nine practices are: reading scripture for formation, hymn singing, Sabbath rest, silent prayer, forgiveness, healing light, integrity, discernment, and hospitality.

1. Reading Scripture for Formation, not Information

As elders, we can become strong, positive spiritual influencers within the life of the congregation by leading out of our own spiritual center. This is the place where we are ourselves nurtured in the heart of God through scripture. We have been trained in our tradition to read the Bible critically and analytically. While this is excellent exercise for the intellect, it may not fully exercise the soul. So instead of reading the Bible to extract data and "get something out of it," we seek to read with the intention of placing ourselves quietly before the Author and allowing scripture to shape and form our consciousness. Isaiah's image of a potter comes to mind (64:8). The ancient church called this *lectio divina,* divine reading. It is letting God's Word read us.

A word of instruction: Settle into a comfortable chair. As you become aware of body stress points, release the tensions. Let go of distractions, take some deep breaths, and center down. Focus on a brief passage of scripture, not more than three to four verses. Read the text slowly several times, allowing key words to come up off the page at you. Hold in your heart those words that seem to shimmer with illumination and repeat them softly to yourself. Whenever you find your attention drifting, simply

---

[3]David Keirsey and Marilyn Bates, *Please Understand Me: Character and Temperament Types* (Del Mar, Calif.: Prometheus Nemesis, 1978).

re-center by repeating the words quietly to yourself. Imagine these words sinking those critical eighteen inches from the mind into the heart. As the mystics say: "When the head sinks into the heart, there is fire!" Stay with these words that blaze like the burning bush, yet are not consumed. Allow these words to abide, letting each facet sparkle like a diamond dancing in special light. Perhaps you have intellectual questions and curiosities about the text you will want to settle later, but for now, rest in the Word you've been given and rejoice in its power to renovate, renew, refresh, restore, redeem, reconcile, and release the grace you most need.

Passages for your practice:

Jeremiah 29:11–14, Proverbs 20:27, Isaiah 43:1–3, Luke 10:41–42, John 20:22–23

Reflections for your journaling:

1. Is there an invitation God's spirit seems to be gently offering you as you surrender yourself to the meaning of passage?
2. If this passage were a drop of rain falling into the soil of your soul, what kind of ground would it be falling on? Can you describe the condition?
3. Take notice of the little curiosities that seem to form around this Word, but be content simply to note them with a key word, leaving them for later exploration.
4. Is there any impression you are left with—almost like a soft footprint on your soul—as you leave this passage?
5. Could there be some internal sense of divine purpose this Word is forming within you?
6. Did you notice how you dealt with mental distractions or restlessness of body?
7. What has this Word freed you from as well as freed you for?

2. Hymn Singing

Perhaps you don't have many "solo voices" in your elders' circle, but you can still sing a new song. We automatically think of music with a performance orientation instead of simply an expression of the soul's adoration. If you can free yourself from self-consciousness, and get into the flow and the poetry, something as basic as group singing is a tried and true way of honoring the Presence among us. Just open the hymnbook and share favorites, singing one another—as the old Shaker tune says—"into the place just right." This can be a beautiful way to enter into the Presence (Ps. 100:2).

A word of instruction: Try to concentrate your singing not so much on hearing your own voice above all the rest, but hearing yours in concert, blending with others. Try not to get caught up in the performance of music to the point that it gets in the way of hearing the internal and eternal song. Adjust your pace and volume so that the song almost feels as though it is singing itself, rather than you consciously forcing your song outward. If you have memories of precious people or moments associated with this hymn, acknowledge them gladly and gratefully and enjoy them without giving them the power to distract you from your main focus: being present for and with God. Make an offering of your song. Once you have found yourself in the Presence, let your singing cease, simple falling away, as you listen to others or enjoy the silence.

Suggested hymns that may especially draw you:

> *CH,* 254, "Breathe on Me, Breath of God"
> *CH,* 111, "Santo, Santo, Santo"
> *CH,* 4, "Holy, Holy, Holy! Lord God Almighty"
> *CH,* 305, "Lord, Listen to Your Children Praying"
> *CH,* 543, "Blessed Assurance"

Reflections for your journaling:

1. How does God's invitation come to you through this song?
2. Are you drawn deeper into the mystery of God because of the particularly haunting lyrics or tune of the hymn?
3. Is there some note buried deep—beneath words and music—that resounds a deep chord within you and draws you through a knothole into a new dimension?
4. What image is evoked here that opens up a whole new dimension of your awareness of God?

3. Sabbath Rest

Elders who can offer peaceful listening and minister a calming influence out of the Sabbath rest in their own souls will be an enormous blessing! When we observe Sabbath, we participate in a biblical work strike, in imitation of the divine Creator, who established a rhythm of six on and one off. Because of the pace of postmodern life, most of us can only bear to practice Sabbath in small doses at a time. As we faithfully pursue this practice though, the rest refreshes the soul (Ps. 23:2).

A word of instruction: Imagine the ruckus it might have caused the first time God went "on strike." Consider how God modeled the highest form of freedom, by giving God's self the liberty to take liberty. Jesus embodied this same spiritual freedom and warned against any legalistic attitudes that encroach upon and bind us to "rules and regulations" around the right way to practice this way into God. If Sabbath is truly "time out to take eternity in," consider what you are taking time out from and what of eternity you are taking into your being. For many of us Sabbath is associated with a place of vacation or moment of relaxation. Can you visit that place? It need not be anywhere exotic or elaborate to be effective in assisting your presence for God. The important thing is that it be readily accessible to your soul's imagination, a place of spirit rest.

Practicing the practice: Please feel the invitation to go to your soul's Sabbath rest space and abide there for a season until you are refreshed. Say to each distraction as it tries to intrude and disturb your rest: Nothing needs to happen now! Perhaps repeating the words of Psalm 46:10 will allow you to enter your resting place. Hush your yammering, stammering mind as you would a gabby, boisterous child. Allow your soul to catch up with your bushed and busy body. Sometimes a change in the pace of our work is almost as good as a vacation, so establish a new rhythm.

Reflections for your journaling:

1. Ever wonder why you have so much trouble getting to this place of untroubled rest?

2. What changes take place in your body as you enter the Sabbath space?

3. What is it like to be who you are, before God, in that place of peace?

4. Ask yourself: Why do I deny my body the soul-rest that is so needed?

5. David danced in sheer delight before the Lord. How do you play in the Presence?

6. Have you ever considered resting and fasting from something besides food? What about a fast from media or noise?

7. What is the least distracting way for you to treat interruptions in your rest?

4. Silent Prayer as a Way into the Presence

One elders' circle I know practices silence together, using that old Quaker line, "feel free to speak if you can improve the silence!" Sometimes, instead of expressing our inner soul condition before God, words get in the way of that expression. We need a rest from words. Silence can help hush the noisy heart and make the quiet a vestibule whereby we enter the Holy of Holies.

A word of instruction: Bring your body to rest in some posture that frees you from restlessness and allows you to be without distraction. Choose a word as your mantra. You may use your favorite, most personal, intimate name for God. Let this word become the centerpiece of your prayer, sinking deeply into its comfort and awe. Whenever you are distracted by noise or mind chatter, simply note what is disturbing your peace and sink beneath it, into the deeper presence of God. The key here is to rest in God while God works in you. Allow yourself the freedom to not force yourself to think anything, do anything, or intend anything. Free yourself in the Spirit from the obligation to feel that something "has to happen" or "not happen" in this time of communion. Just let be....

Practicing the practice: Give yourself permission to set aside the alarm clock or egg timer and enjoy God's presence.

After all, this is not swimming practice—you are not being graded on how long you can hold your breath or how long you can notice God. This time is a little space hollowed out of eternity to allow eternity's impact on your soul. This is a "time out" in order to take eternity in. You may wish to use the lyrics of that old Beatles tune as a way in: "When I find myself in times of trouble, Mother Mary comes to me…there will be an answer, let it be." Or the words of John Greenleaf Whittier:

> And so, I find it well to come
> For deeper rest to this still room,
> For here the habit of the soul
> Feels less the outer world's control.
> The strength of mutual purpose pleads
> More earnestly our common needs.
> And from the silence multiplied
> By these still forms on either side
> The world that time and sense have known
> Falls off and leaves us God alone![4]

Reflections for your journaling:

1. How did the silence sit with you? Is it well with your soul?
2. Can you identify any points of discomfort or struggle that broke your concentration?
3. Do you find yourself moving toward being able to tolerate stillness and silence for progressively longer and more restful times?
4. Is there any sense of moving from a very self-conscious "timing your silence" to a wider awareness of "timeless time" or the in-breaking of eternity?
5. Are you beginning to allow background noises to simply slip or glide by, without feeling as though you have to attach your attention to each one and give it the power of a full-fledged distraction?

---

[4]John Greenleaf Whittier, "The Meeting," found online in July, 2003, at www.kimopress.com/whittier.htm.

6. Can you find a resting place within the silence that is truly the heart of God for you?
7. Would you allow yourself to remain there for a season just enjoying God?
8. Are you able to use your sacred word as a touchstone to help you return to your sense of the Presence when your silence is disrupted?

5. Forgiveness

The capacity of the elders to practice forgiveness, particularly among themselves, changes the temperature of any congregation, melts barriers to growth, opens opportunity, and pours spiritual energy into relationships. The inverse is also operative! Sometimes our souls are so depressed and weighted down by the sheer magnitude of unforgiveness among us that it affects the climate within the congregation and creates heavy weather!

As Jesus left the upper room, he prayed that a spirit of unity would prevail (John 17), and after the resurrection, "he breathed on them and said to them, 'Receive the Holy Spirit. If you forgive the sins of any, they are forgiven them; if you retain the sins of any, they are retained'" (Jn. 20:22–23).

Elders, we cannot be a reconciling force within our congregations unless we are reconciled and reconciling souls ourselves. As one elder bluntly stated it: For better or for worse, we are the agents of reconciliation within this congregation (paraphrase of 2 Cor. 5:16–20). An implication follows: If we have hostility unresolved among us, how can we offer peace to others? Practicing forgiveness in the elders' circle requires courage to confess, which makes us vulnerable to others. One of the most helpful ways to get at this dynamic is Lewis Smedes's little parable of the "Magic Eyes," in his book *A Pretty Good Person.*[5]

A word of instruction: Give each elder in your circle a small pebble to hold as someone reads aloud Smedes's parable. Imagine the pebble you are holding represents the weight of

---

[5]Lewis Smedes, *A Pretty Good Person: What It Takes to Live with Courage, Gratitude, and Integrity, or, When Pretty Good Is as Good as You Can Be* (San Francisco: Harper & Row, 1990).

judgment and not giving forgiveness or being forgiven. Does your pebble have a name or represent a situation that is still stuck in your craw? Ask God to teach you about the meaning of this parable as it touches your life and the elders with whom you are eldering.

Reflections for your journaling:

1. What would reconciliation look like in this relationship? What does the bottom line cost?
2. What in you stubbornly resists reconciliation?
3. What would be the worst thing that could happen if you made the first move to reconcile with your pebble person?
4. How important is it for you to feel safe while you work this relationship out? How might your eldership provide this same safety net to others in the congregation as they work out their own salvation with fear and trembling?
5. How can we best support one another in this, the hardest of all eldering tasks?
6. What might Matthew 18:18–22 mean in this context?
7. Is the Holy Spirit an active part of your forgiving process, and how might you call on the Spirit for assistance?
8. What does it mean to practice forbearance after the forgiveness?

6. Healing Light

We have all been so turned off by the caricatures of healing evangelists who slap people down with the $20 blessing. These cartoons are so repulsive that we avoid any appearance of interest in healing, but elders cannot ignore the overwhelming needs for healing in our hurting world and in the wider church family and community. We can offer hope through the healing ministry of intercessory prayer and practicing the ancient arts of sacramental healing as well. The critical thing to remember is that the Spirit of the Lord is our healer. It is not about us.

A word of instruction: Our traditional Disciples rationalistic assumptions about the nature of God's healing work are challenged on a practical level when it comes to both charismatic and sacramental forms of healing. Perhaps the place to begin is a radical reread of James 5:13–17. The practice of the early church was to invite the elders to visit homes and offer prayers for healing, accompanied by a laying on of hands and an anointing with oil. You would be surprised how many Disciples congregations already quietly practice this ritual of home communion and healing prayers. Disciples have worked out an informal theology of healing that flows out of our deep sense of God's presence and power at the table. We know Christ is present in loving and healing ways whenever we break bread. Why would God's healing light and love, so powerfully witnessed in bread and cup, not also be available (perhaps "sacramentally," but however God chooses) through anointing with oil, laying on elders' hands, and praying?

We do not need a systematic theology of healing, with all the irrational kinks worked out, before we practice the offering of God's mercy for those among us who are most needy. We simply invite the healing wholeness Christ ministered on earth to be present for those we love and serve. Disciples elders can learn much of the basic understandings necessary to conduct a healing prayer ministry through reading Agnes Sanford, who conducted schools of pastoral care for Episcopalians for years. Her work taught many priests the how-to of healing prayer. Her modern UCC counterpart would be Dr. Flora Wuellner, whose retreat work and books are well known among Disciples. The work of spiritual writers from Upper Room ministries is especially useful. For a practical guide in setting up healing prayer networks, I recommend the work of James Wagner.[6]

Practicing the practice:

1. Just like the friends of the paralytic who lowered their dear one down through the roof to present his needs at Jesus' feet, you can begin by holding the one whose health and well-being is of great concern to you before the healing light of Christ. Imagine this Light shining in glory on him or her,

---

[6]James Wagner, *Blessed to Be a Blessing* (Nashville: Upper Room, 1980).

bathing the person, flowing down and coming to rest on particular portions of the body that might be most in need of the healing Presence. Take your time; do not rush this prayer.

2. Thank God for everything that only God can do and is doing for this person you hold dear.

3. Ask the Spirit of God, who according to Romans 8 teaches us how to pray, to pray those prayers through you that need praying. Offer yourself as a channel for this divine blessing.

4. After some season of practice, if you do not seem to find a greater degree of comfort with this prayer, feel free to intercede for others' healing in the ways God gives you to pray for them. There is no need to degrade yourself if this is not your gift, nor is it necessary to deride others to whom it has been given to pray in this or any number of other ways. The ways of the Spirit are decent and orderly, but not necessarily orthodox in a traditional sense. Ask God how God would have you do this work of healing prayer for your flock. Ways unique to your own relationship to God may unfold for you as you listen and let God lead.

Reflections for your journaling:

1. What changes did you notice in yourself as you offered prayers in this way?

2. What would have to be significantly shifted inside of you to offer this healing prayer for your enemies? Are there some blocks and barriers you can name?

3. Did you sense any invitation of God in the midst of your prayers?

4. How does the Spirit intercede for us?

5. Is there such a thing as a prayer beyond words? (See Jude 20 or Eph. 6:18.)

7. Integrity: The Walk of All Our Talk

Disciples congregations will never rise above the level of spiritual commitment the elders offer through the integrity of example. So how can we as elders raise this ceiling to a new level? The folks of our flocks are looking to us for practical, lived-out Christian lives, not perfect lives, but they rightly expect us to be souls who are sensitive to the chinks and gaps, and do not excuse or ignore them. They need to see us sweat as we work out our own salvation with fear and trembling. Authenticity is another name for the spiritual transparency that says: "Yes, I have my problems and blind spots too, but I am working on them, and they are working on me! However humbling my humanity may be to bear at times, I still believe 'that the one who began a good work [in me] will bring it to completion by the day of Jesus Christ'" (Phil. 1:6).

A word of instruction: Take a long look in the mirror, and especially the mirror of God's Word, Hebrews 4:11. Can you imagine what the people of your congregation see when they look at your life? What would someone sitting in the pews see in you? Are there any areas of obvious, glaring discrepancy? Can you identify any broken spots where Christ might be calling you out of inward dividedness into a new measure of wholeness? Have you taken a stroll through the shadow side of your life lately? How is the Spirit healing your double-mindedness about certain sins of which you have formerly been oblivious? Is there within your spiritual backbone a single-mindedness that wills with *one, undivided will* to do God's will?

Practicing the practice: There is nowhere this searching out of our integrity becomes more painful than in our personal stewardship practices as elders. If you have not read Rhodes Thompson's classic book *Stewards Shaped by Grace*,[7] by all means do.

Rhodes raises difficult questions about whether our personal practices in the stewardship area bear up under spiritual scrutiny. Here is a matter of utmost integrity. Many elders think their personal stewardship is "an intensely private matter between them and their God." Perhaps people in the pews can hide behind this

---

[7]Rhodes Thompson, *Stewards Shaped by Grace* (St. Louis: Chalice Press, 1990).

rationalization, but elders know better. After you have been an elder a few years, everybody around you can guess within a hundred dollars how seriously you take your personal stewardship. This may seem like an exaggeration until you think about the ways our lives as spiritual leaders are an open secret. People know! As elders, we telegraph our integrity about tithing just by the way we squirm when the subject comes up. Perhaps tithing doesn't come up often enough. The kingdom's cause is beleaguered and hurting for financial support because we have not examined our leadership role as elders. We need more congregations in which the spiritual leadership has taken on the mission of tithing as a matter of spiritual integrity.

Imagine what would happen if it were understood that all those holding the ancient and honorable office of elder were either practicing tithing (as a floor, not as a ceiling) or were practicing a form of systematic stewardship growth through proportionate giving that had them on a timetable to become tithers long before they died. If all this seems too harsh or legalistically demanding, consider this: If the elders of a congregation won't tithe as a matter of integrity, who will? No congregation will ever rise above the example of integrity set by its elder leadership.

Reflections for your journaling:

1. Is this matter of tithing a serious challenge to the integrity of your elder leadership? Are you willing to counsel and consider some sort of plan that could help you move from where you are to where you would yet like to be? For instance, many elders tithe their estate to the church. Are you at least willing to take on a season of prayer and discernment to discover God's call for your life and leadership in this matter? If you are unwilling to step up to this consideration, should you think seriously about stepping down?

2. Whom can you trust to talk through this matter among your elder-colleagues? Who in your elder circle could be a prayer partner as you courageously examine your conscience and

work through your concerns? Who could "elder" you through this critical stage of your growth as a spiritual leader?
3. Have you gotten past trying to be the perfect example? Can you laugh about how overrated perfection is because it turns far too much attention back on the ego?
4. Do you really believe in the power of spiritual example, or is this just a concept to which you nod allegiance?
5. If you are a tither already, how is God leading you to make a verbal witness about this practice among the elders and congregation? How can this witness not end up being about me, but about the grace of surrender that makes this gift possible? Can you come at this task from the mode of praise?

8. Discernment

Congregations need spiritual leaders who will lead by bringing the full power of their collective wisdom to bear on the issues and problems of the day. The elders' circle can be a place where elders ask: What is God saying to us at this turn in the road? Sometimes this guidance will unfold in consensual ways through discussion, listening in silence, and group prayer. Other times individual elders may be led to offer a witness of what the Spirit seems to be saying to them. Still other moments may call for a prophetic word to be spoken in the circle, which becomes a place of collective sifting and sorting of God's intention among us. Perhaps problem solving and administrative tasks can be left for committees and boards, while elders give themselves to this kind of prayer and serving the Word.

A word of instruction: The work of spiritual discernment is a prayerful, intentional attempt to sift and sort, to distinguish the heart of God and the word of the Spirit amidst the many voices that may be competing for our conscious attention. This is more than mere problem solving on a rational level. It involves loving the questions, not just grasping for the answers. This is not to abandon or ignore sound logical and rational analysis based on the best available information. The discernment process traditionally carries the answers of the mind deeper into the heart. Here we humbly acknowledge that the heart has answers the mind knows not of. So we seek both to answer our questions and question our answers as we embrace and engage the totality of our being–our senses, feelings, intuitions, and imaginations. The goal of this process is to seek out the mind of Christ for the matter at hand (Phil. 2:5). At one level, we are asking the question of Charles Sheldon's immensely popular book *In His Steps*: what would Jesus do? (WWJD)

At another level the equally important question may be: What is God already doing? (WIGAD) Perhaps the fingerprints of the Spirit's present activity are at least as important to discern as God's footsteps behind us in the sand! Discernment is a process of walking together, listening, and praying until a "way opens." This is a process of continual commitment to remain in community and connection, talking and walking together. Dr. Robert Hill of Community Christian Church in Kansas City is fond of quoting the saying "We make the way by walking."

Practicing the practice: It is not difficult to identify an issue or sticky circumstance in the life of your congregation that is radically in need of God's gift of discernment. Perhaps the first question is: Is this the time for this matter to come before the congregation? Here we seek the distinction between matters that are the heartbeat of our life with God from something that is merely urgent. As you sit in silence, make a prayer of invitation, asking the inner light to emerge and illumine your heart in this matter. As you begin, you may also want to express gratitude to God for any bit of illumination that the Spirit may offer to shine on this concern. You may also become aware, through praise and thanks, of the ways God is already shedding light on this matter. You may wish to begin giving witness to these nuances of light among you. You may want to check out your obedience to the light already manifest in your midst. Sometimes we don't get any more guidance until we do something with the guidance already given. Listening with a mind to obey God and fiercely follow the light is a good place to begin discernment.

I invite you to work your way through a simple guided meditation based on Psalm 1:4. "Chaff that the wind drives away." Use your sanctified imagination to think of the matter before you for discernment as a head of grain, lying on some ancient, biblical-times threshing floor as oxen trample it under hoof. (See how stomping around helps separate the wheat from the chaff?) Now imagine this grain, wheat and chaff, being hoisted up by winnowing forks into the mighty winds that blow through the threshing floor at harvest time. (Instead of tossing our hands up and quitting, let's toss our problems up, trusting them to the winds of God's spirit.) As gusts drive the chaff away, the kernels drop heavily to the floor and are gathered, sifted, and ground into a wonderful wheat bread that will nourish the community. You may want to continue for some time in this meditative mode, playing with these images as a way of intuitively working through this problem.

Reflections for your journaling:

1. What kinds of comments encourage and help create an atmosphere in your elders' circle that affirms your desire to intentionally seek the mind of Christ in crucial matters?
2. Is it ever okay in your elders' circle to stop discussion dead-in-its-tracks? A "time out" for prayer in the middle of the debate might shift the conversation to a deeper level. What would happen if you simply called for a "moment of silence" followed by a season of sentence prayer around the circle?
3. Why might we as elders resist or utilize this approach in our decision-making process?
4. How does the Word inform our opinions and options?

9. Hospitality

Elders are not only the prayer hosts at the Lord's table but also hosts and embodiers of God's loving, welcoming ways. This is far more than simply "saying hello and making nice" with first-time church visitors. When you see a young mother struggling with a baby on one hip and balancing two plates in the fellowship dinner line, don't wonder who will help her find an empty seat and a highchair; it's your calling as an elder! When you see a stranger darken the door, don't turn to ask a friend, "Who's that?"

Follow your first and most generous impulse: Extend your hand and introduce yourself. Initiating the ministry of acceptance and grace is one of the major ways elders "eld." Our churches need an outbreak of this attitude; it needs to be contagious.

A word of instruction: Invest some silent time living your way into the meaning of Romans 15:7. How would you describe the ways Christ has welcomed you into the heart of God? What would it look like if your congregation extended this same spirit and attitude inside the four walls of your church as well as outside the four walls in the larger community? Where do you draw the motivational power to want to reach out to strangers in our xenophobic society?

Now clear your mind and heart for some centering-down prayer. Use this phrase from Luke 10:41–42 as your focal point for a time of meditation: " (insert your own name here, repeat it twice), you are worried and distracted by many things; there is need of only one thing."

Stay with this thought, repeating the phrase as often as necessary to keep you focused and praying.

Reflections for your journaling:

1. Consider the ways Christ lived out the spirit of welcome in his dealings with strangers. (John 4)
2. Have you ever entertained an angel, aware or unaware? (Heb. 13:2)
3. How might hospitality be a call to integrate our "Martha mode" with our "Mary mode"? (Lk. 10:38–42).
4. Reflect on hospitality as the fundamental shift in consciousness that allows us to hollow out a space for God that leads to the hollowing out of space for another person.
5. How is the heart of God warmed by your welcome?
6. Have you considered the difference between a pilgrim and a stranger?
7. How is spiritual befriendment not about being an "off-the-chart" extrovert?

The Outpouring of an Elder's Life

When Times Get Tough

Elders in today's church bear the primary weight of responsibility for the spiritual well-being of the congregation. Pastors will come and go, but elders remain the "leaders on the spot." In the good times, elders gladly collaborate with their pastors through seasons of spiritual vitality and joy. However, in times of storm and controversy, elders are the designated local leaders who must step up to the helm and guide the ship. This is not a time for timidity, whatever our personal trepidations. When stormy dangers threaten the safety and well-being of the congregation, someone is in charge of doing something–the elders. A study of Paul's final charge to the Ephesian elders (Acts 20:17–38) might provide an excellent introduction about how to weather tough times. Another practical aid would be skillful training in conflict management. The best time to schedule this work is during a season of relatively smooth sailing. Elders need to know their strengths and limitations in the heat of conflict. Summoning the spiritual courage, as well as learning the good timing, helps elders step into the fray at the critical moment.

That is the silent moment of gasp and breathlessness when the weight of accusation is finally "out on the table." Something needs to happen in the moment–timing is everything!

I am always amazed at how many relatively minor controversies escalate into full-blown conflicts because good elders did nothing, said nothing, and just sat there. We need to learn the fine art of throwing our bodies into this gap. In this moment of shock, when everyone is horrified and hopes someone else will say something quick, there is someone in charge of speaking up and speaking out–the elders. Of course, there will always be "personality clashes" and "differences of opinion." These may be dealt with in charity and graciousness. I am speaking of the dynamic operative that allows these kinds of things to get out of hand. All that evil needs to cast its shadow across the congregation is for good elders to become paralyzed and do nothing. Learning what to do, how to do it, and how to intercede in the prayerful sense as well as the political sense is incumbent on the eldership. Parallel to what may be happening in the physical realm, an attack may be occurring in the spiritual realm. Elders need to know how to discern the signs of movement in this realm. Most elders experience the power of evil to inflict wounds and lodge accusations that stick and do damage to souls, but they do not know how to counteract this situation in prayer and the realm of the Spirit. The congregation needs its mature elders to step into battle. Spiritual warfare must be waged by elders and intercessors who understand and can operate in this realm of eternal reality.

Elders who don't know how to put on the whole armor of God (Eph. 6:10–18) are going to be brutalized and sidelined in the conflict. Admittedly, some of our elders are irenic spirits– that's why they were chosen. Irenic spirits need to recognize they may not be much help in the heat of battle, but they can support and cheer those who are leading the charge. Some of our elders are warrior spirits who instinctively operate in this realm and thrive on crisis. This is why every congregation needs the whole community of the elders' circle to lead them. Regardless of temperament, all elders bear the responsibility to recognize what is going on and work and pray for what Ephesians 4:3 calls "the unity of the Spirit in the bond of peace." It takes every elder bearing his or her full share of the weight to carry the congregation through stormy times.

Learning to Operate as an Elders' Circle through Accountability, Agreement, and Intercession

The most effective elders groups I know are those who have learned by trial and error that they really do need one another—in all the diversity of gifts, temperaments, and personalities—in order to enjoy the fullest measure of spiritual satisfaction this servant leader calling affords. Practically speaking, this means that eldering is not "lone ranger" work. We are a minibody of the larger body of the congregation. If the congregation is ever going to live, love, and witness as a body, it will be because elders have learned how to live out this unity in their circle and how to extend this reign of God into the congregation. We must forge clear understandings of at least three principals to guide the formation of the basis on which we operate as a body. They are accountability, agreement, and intercession.

Accountability

In the workplace, we practice accountability whether we agree with the boss or not. The corporate world's power to "hire and fire" keenly focuses our sense of responsibility and loyalty. In volunteer organizations such as the church, we often try to adopt this corporate style with mixed results. We do need a place where the buck stops. In most Disciples churches, no matter what our constitution and bylaws may say, our practice is to locate this buck-stopping power in the office of the chair of the board and the senior pastor. They serve in our polity as the two leading spiritual and administrative leaders of the congregation. Unity and progress depend on their working relationship, which is generally built around the concept of mutual accountability. We need this same quality of mutual connection among our elders. Ever since the functional committee system was adopted among

Disciples congregations in the 1960s, the elders have felt misplaced, dislodged in the structure, and a bit confused about what to do and where they belong. Subsequently the crucial energy of their leadership has been lost in the shuffle, which often places a premium on efficient administration. Elders' circles that learn to operate as a body can work on the quality of corporate life through practicing accountability.

Accountability is the single-minded willingness to live a high-quality Christian life in thought, word, and deed with a high degree of spiritual integration and maturity. Integrity is transparent congruence in attitude and action. It manifests in a consistency that moves toward wholeness and holiness. Single-mindedness, as described by Kierkegaard, means to "will with one will to do the will of God." In other words: not double-minded. James literally describes this split condition as "double souled" (Jas. 1:7). Jesus named this attitude as "serving two masters" (Mt. 6:24). Double-mindedness desires two things at once—leading to split consciousness, a split conscience—and drives a wedge between words and deeds. In the split between "what we say we believe" and "what we do after we say that"—most of us have spent the most uncomfortable moments of our lives!

We long to live according to our best intentions, choosing a whole-souled approach that makes conformity to the life of Christ our norm. We inevitably miss this mark, which unsettles us no end. However, sinless perfectionism is vastly overrated That is, it ends up being all about us! Any aspect of our ego that is unsurrendered to the Spirit and not in conformity to the crucified Christ can quickly co-opt even our highest and best intentions and twist them narcissistically inward. Even something as sacred as a quest for spiritual excellence easily becomes "all about me" instead of "all about Christ in me, the hope of glory." The goal of the Christian life is not sinlessness but wholeness, health, and well-being in the image of Christ. Sinlessness is not a state of consciousness at which we finally arrive, but a daily process of conformity to Christ, who continually yielded to a higher purpose and higher power beyond his own.

While it is true that final completion of our salvation is a blessing reserved for the life of the world to come, this does not mean we can afford to live lives of careless spirituality that are undisciplined, standing uncorrected and unconnected to the faith community.

In the words of Paul, we "press on toward the goal for the prize of the heavenly call of God in Christ Jesus" (Phil. 3:14). We humbly seek to fulfill the image of God created in us through birth, which is continually being recreated in us through rebirth. This process of reconciliation and healing is a lifelong one. This is our intentionally chosen path. This is the way of Christ. Our lives, before God and humankind, will inevitably have their share of failures, fumbles, and flops. We sin and miss the mark of our high calling in Christ Jesus, but we never lose sight of our spiritual destiny: to live our life courageously and wholeheartedly before God and before others. This means continual confession to God and to one another. This means we submit to the counsel, encouragement, guidance, and help of the full circle of elders as we seek to live in the unity and community of the Spirit. This means our failures are open to the kind of constructive criticism that will build us up in Christ. This can occur through speaking the truth in love. This means when we are "overtaken in a fault," those who mutually share our highest spiritual intention must be relied on to restore us, gently, graciously, and humbly to full faith, recognizing that their turn in the "hot seat" is next! Forging spiritual partnerships in which pilgrims bond together means we must devise strategies that lift and carry one another over the common stumbling spots on the journey. This is the point of accountability. It is not spiritual voyeurism that enjoys armchair quarterbacking somebody else's game! It is not a harsh, competitive rivalry that judges the faults of others and "one-ups" them. It is an unrelenting willingness to submit my practice of my faith to those who practice faith with me.

Among Disciples, we hold such a privatistic view of Christianity that we are, by and large, extremely reluctant to invite one another into the space where we live "God alone." This is considered "too private to broach." Only slowly do we learn our humble interdependence. Only sadly do we recognize Cain's question as our own. This mutuality is the only way we can live true to Christ and fulfill our leadership of God's flock, being spiritually accountable to one another as elders. This means breaking more than bread. It requires the breaking open of our lives before God and before one another. I will be the first to admit that exposing ourselves to the light of God is painful enough alone, but in the company of others it is excruciating. Yet this very word *excruciating* contains the root meaning "out of the crucifix," and only out of the power of the cross can we truly live the life God intended anyway.

What does accountability look like in the elders' circle? Perhaps it involves choosing a partner in whose friendship we see the face of God, and inviting them to remind us of what we say we most want: to live in the heart of God. Then invite them not to simply point out those self-defeating ways in which we are not living in that sacred space, but to help us explore our powerful resistance to repentance and change. Instead of just reading us the riot act and punishing us for our failure to be what we say we most want to be (which is pretty much the way we expect to be treated after we have messed up), mutual accountability means supporting our desire for a new life with God by drawing us toward grace and helping us be restored to shalom, the reign of God's peace. The organizing principle of spiritual accountability is the word of Jesus that as we know the truth, it sets us free! So we agree to speak the truth to one another in love and trust that God will get that truth where it needs to be, to have the transforming effect God intends.

Agreement

Barbara Brown Taylor, in her book *Speaking of Sin,* describes grace as "not only that infinite supply of divine forgiveness, but the mysterious strength that keeps turning us toward God and powering our desire for the restoration of our relationship to God."[1] When this grace is at work as accountability within the elders' circle, it sets the stage for spiritual agreement to unfold. The organizing principle here is the word of Jesus in Matthew 18:18–20, regarding being of one mind in a purpose God reveals. Sometimes we come up against our own resistance to God's intention and need to talk it through in a relationship of trust. Other times we delight in the fresh revelation of divine purpose and need prayer support as we collaborate with God in a purpose God intends. Quite often this involves boldly asking for the faith to bring into the human realm the vision we have seen in prayer. Spiritual agreement is not so much a meeting of the minds as it is a discovery of the ever-present oneness of our hearts before God.

In this area the unique contribution Disciples have made to ecumenical dialogue can be applied in a practical way to church life. By the gift and grace of faith, the congregation is already one in a purpose that serves God. This unity is confirmed by our common study of scripture, and is experienced in seasons of contemplation. Sometimes little signs, convergences, serendipities, and coincidences occur around our prayers and watchful discernment. We may also touch this reality in deep moments of worship or find this shalom in seasons of prayer. Our oneness with the purpose of God in the spiritual realm is realized in time and space whenever we, by faith, recognize what God desires, claim what God desires, give thanks for its unfolding, and then set our hands to this work of the heart.

This is the essential meaning of Jesus' word: "If two of you agree on earth about anything you ask, it will be done for you by my Father in heaven" (Mt. 18:19). Far from seeking carte blanche wish fulfillment, or engaging in Christmas list praying, we become partners in the creative purpose of God–the in-breaking of the kingdom. Agreement in prayer around a discerned purpose God intends seems to give God an open channel through which to

---

[1]Barbara Brown Taylor, *Speaking of Sin* (Cambridge/Boston: Cowley, 2000), 85.

accomplish divine purpose. We become conduits of the creative purpose of God in the world. When elders pray together in this kind of accord, spiritual power is unleashed and dark forces are bound. The spiritual realities of the kingdom, power, and glory that Jesus taught us to attend in the Lord's Prayer, come to earth, "as they already are in heaven." Elders who stand shoulder-to-shoulder and heart-to-heart in the prayer circle are channels for the "good things that keep happening" in the congregation. This is the work of the Spirit, and great cause for rejoicing!

Intercession

While the elders in any given congregation may be from widely diverse cultural backgrounds, the common discovery through prayer is that it is only the kingdom culture that counts. That is to say, our unity is not based on "being alike." It is not even based on "thinking alike" or liking the same things. (This applies to everything from dress code in the congregation to style of worship.) The basis of the elders' unity as the core congregational leadership is the discernment of a fundamental spiritual reality: We already are the one body of Christ in the world. (This is true even when we do not discern it!) Out of this grounding in our *one*ness in Christ, we recognize and greet with joy the presence of the Holy Spirit in one another. This Spirit makes our intercessions as elders possible and effective. Paul put it this way, sometimes "we do not know how to pray as we ought, but that very Spirit intercedes with sighs too deep for words" (Rom. 8:26). Elders find ways to present themselves to the Lord as servants of the Spirit in the realm of prayer. Elders are willing to enter into the depths of prayer, holding themselves simply open to God and spiritual communion. Through the grace of confession and forgiveness, elders become fit and worthy vessels for God to pour out spiritual energy into the life of the congregation. This power may express itself in many forms: blessing, encouragement, healing, insight into problem solving, containment of bad attitudes, restraint of gossip, articulation of appropriate boundaries, comfort and counsel, anointing for inspirational moments in leadership and worship—and many more!

Elders' prayers become part of the spiritual channel through which these graces unfold in our congregational life. The exact rational meaning of these spiritual realities remains a mystery. Even so famous a biblical scholar among us as Fred Craddock puzzles over the meaning of the instruction found in Jude 20 and Ephesians 6:18 to pray in the Spirit.[2] Perhaps God's own great heart is praying a continuous prayer for the wholeness, health, salvation, and well-being of God's beloved creation. Elders have the privilege of entering into this sacred sanctuary of the universe when we are willing to intercede for those purposes God places on our hearts. Simply put, God has many prayers that God wants to pray through us, and when we place ourselves at the disposal of the Holy Spirit, we allow those prayers to be prayed and those purposes to come to fruition in the providence of God. We pray to God and on behalf of God, in order that God's will unfold on earth as it already has unfolded in heaven. Intercession brings heaven to earth.

Elders are spiritual leaders who learn how to give their hearts to God for this purpose. We claim no uncanny capacity to "make things happen" in the realm of prayer; we only strap on the full armor of God, in the language of Ephesians 6:10–18, and enter into warfare as we are directed by discernment and agreement. It is always *such* a wake-up call when elders discover their true heart's calling in intercessory prayer. All the clamoring anxiety over what elders are "supposed to do" finally falls away, and the elders' true vocation arises to claim us. If elders in our Disciples churches did nothing more in this millennium than recover their hearts for God in prayer, it would be enough to revitalize our congregations. Prayer makes all the difference in this world...and the next!

---

[2]Fred Craddock, *First and Second Peter and Jude,* Westminster Bible Companion (Louisville: Westminster John Knox Press, 1995), 147.

The Eternal Work of Elders

In the apocalyptic writing of John of Patmos, we find a glimpse of the eternal work of the elders. Following the word of the Spirit to the churches in Revelation 2 and 3, the scene shifts to the throne of God in heaven. Here a powerful vision of glory and praise, constantly and eternally offered to God, sweeps the reader up into an eternal dimension beyond time and space. The heart of worship orders the universe. Surrounding God's presence are the four beasts, representing the entire created order. The twenty-four elders (twelve Old Testament tribes and twelve New Testament apostles) symbolize the whole people of God. The work of the elders is aptly described as "falling down" (Rev. 5:8) and pouring out the prayers of the saints before the Almighty.

It strikes me that an elder's work is to help present the prayers of the church before the majesty of God. How everlastingly odd! Of all the many dimensions of eldering we have tried to trace in such careful detail, the only aspect that even gets an honorable mention in the apocalypse is prayer and praise. Is it possible that when we are finally done parsing these paragraphs, the eternal work of elders is simply to embody the triumph of God? Perhaps like the seventy disciples Jesus sent forth in Luke 10, elders do not go about issuing citations for violations; they simply announce with their lives the glad gospel of God's love that wins our sad and broken souls. Perhaps through prayer and praise, elders become the very mercy that holds all creation "near to the heart of God."

The last sentence of this chapter captures my imagination: "And the elders fell down and worshiped" (Rev. 5:14). First, I find more than a little humor in this line, because critical members of the congregation are always beating up on the elders and saying, "They're falling down on their job." But what if their job is falling down? Not on the job, but before the Holy One?

Second, suppose that when all is said and done about eldering in today's postmodern church at the beginning of this new millennium, the only thing that eternally matters is attending the prayer and praise of God? Think how radical the practice of this concept would be. Our elders become no earthly good, because they are swept up in heaven's bidding. Could it be that "taking care of business" and "dealing with administrative matters" ultimately ends up being not all that important in the eternal scheme of things? What if our practice of eldering in the church on earth has not adequately prepared us for our eternal assignment? Maybe we need to turn our practice upside down in order to start living our way into our eternal work of adoration and praise.

Third, let our imagination carry us further. What would happen in our churches if the elders got a head start on our eternal assignment? Since elders are going to attend this work anyway, what if we started now? Suppose our elders took more "time out" to "take eternity in"? What if Wesley got it right: "till we cast our crowns before thee, lost in wonder, love, and praise!"[3] Why not get lost now?

This is a plea for contemplative eldering, an encouragement to become a circle, a community of practice. Elders, God will raise up out of the pews good souls to do all the other work you are currently attending that seems so all-fired important. Your eternal work begins *now* by attending the prayer and praise of God! Ready? Set? Fall on your face!

---

[3]Charles Wesley, "Love Divine, All Loves Excelling," *CH,* 517.